I0016114

eBay 2020

Why You're Not Selling Anything, and What You Can Do About It

Table of Contents

About this book

I will show you how to make money selling on eBay.
Nick Vulich

I know what you're thinking — another book about how to sell on eBay.

Big deal, right?

Trust me. I know how frustrating it is to find reliable information about how to sell online. Everyone says they've created a system, or they can show you exactly what to do to make a profit. I've been there.

I remember when I first started selling on eBay. That was back in the Wild West days of the site when everything was new and uncharted. I didn't know what to do, and no one who could tell me what to do or how to do it. It all came down to poke and hope. I tried a little bit of this, a little bit of that, and hoped things would work out.

That was nearly twenty-years-ago. eBay was just a baby then, and I was a kid learning the ropes.

Today, I know a lot more about selling on eBay. More than most folks, I reckon. But guess what? It's all changing. Just when you think you've got it all down, eBay goes and rewrites the rules. Every six months, they publish a seller update that creates a mad scramble as sellers try to catch up.

Let me tell you this if you don't like change, or if you're afraid of change, selling on eBay most likely isn't going to be for you. The best thing you can do is stop reading this book and request a refund. If, on the other hand, you're up for a wild ride, hitch up your drawers, and let's get started.

I'm not going to go into the mechanics of selling on eBay. There are already a lot of good books out there that tell you how to put a listing together. If you want to learn more, a good starting point is my book, **eBay Unleashed: A Beginners Guide to Selling on eBay** or Ann Eckhart's **Beginner's Guide to Selling on eBay**.

....

Here's the cold hard truth. Less than forty percent of the items listed on eBay sell on the first go around. A few more sell on the second or third run through the wringer. The rest of those items never sell.

Keep that information in the back of your head as you read on. At least half of the stuff you list on eBay won't sell. Ain't gonna happen.

And do you want to know the big reason they don't sell?

It's because of you!

Maybe, you decided to sell the wrong product. Or, you asked for too much money. Or, you wrote a lame-ass description or posted a bunch of sucky pictures. Or, you didn't take the time to position yourself as the best person to sell the item.

Shame on you.

If you want to be successful on eBay, you need to respect the Four Ps.

- **Product**.

    Although it's been said many times that you can sell anything on eBay, that's only half-true. You can sell almost anything on eBay—if it's something somebody wants.

    If you want to make money today—you need to list products people want, need, and are willing to pay for. For example, an iPhone is going to sell quicker than a bucket of nails—unless you're lucky enough to find that one carpenter who's got to have a bucket of nails—NOW.

- **Price**.

Sometimes on eBay, it seems as if we're all engaged in a race to the bottom.

One seller lists an item for a buck. Another seller lists the same thing for 99 cents. The next seller at 98 cents, and so it goes.

In the book world, some eBayers start every book at a penny or 99-cents. Other sellers list every book for $50.00, or $100.00. They both make sales.

So, who is right?

It depends. If you want to sell that book today, the guy selling it for a penny, or 99-cents, is going to have a better chance to sell his item today. If you want to make the most money from each-and-every item you sell, the guy who sells them for fifty or a hundred bucks is going to do better. But he may have to wait six months, or maybe even six years to find a buyer.

How long are you willing to wait to make that sale?

- **Pitch**.

So many sellers don't take the time to think out their item description. They say I have a green shirt, size XXL, and leave it at that.

They don't tell you the brand, or whether it's dark green, light green, or striped. They overlook the big stain on the right side of the hole in the left sleeve.

If you want to sell something, you need to describe it accurately. You need to share the good, the bad, and the ugly. Some people won't buy your shirt because of the stain, or the hole in the sleeve.

That's okay.

A good description helps to weed out the lookers from the buyers. It narrows the playing field down so that you can get to the perfect buyer—FASTER. It will help you find the guy who's looking for an XXL, dark green shirt, with a hole in the left sleeve, and a big old stain on the right-hand side.

Not the best example.

But you get the idea. Your description should help potential buyers fill in the blanks. It should help take them to yes—no—or maybe.

- **Position**.

Position is a little bit product, and a little bit you.

Sometimes you need to tell buyers why they need to buy your product, what they can do with it, or why they need it.

Just as important is you.

Why are you the best guy to sell them the product? Are you an acknowledged expert? A leading retailer? An inventor? Or a product knowledge specialist?

When I sold magazine articles on eBay, everyone and his brother sold the same item for five or ten bucks. I charged twenty-five dollars, or more—and people paid it. They paid it because I positioned myself as a product expert.

I wrote articles about book collecting and vintage magazines. I specialized in my product line and carried over 15,000 collectibles in my inventory—day in, and day out.

I knew my shit. (Pardon my French) No one had any doubts that I was an expert in Nineteenth and Twentieth-Century Paper Americana Collectibles.

I lived and breathed my product line.

How about you?

Have you positioned yourself as a product expert in the line you sell? If not, what's keeping you from getting started?

Get the Four P's right, and you will make a lot of money. Misfire on any of them, and you're doomed to be one of those forty percent sellers we talked about earlier.

It's your choice.

Take the easy road and just get by. Or, hop on the superhighway to eBay selling success

Enough gloom and doom. Let's talk about how to sell and market your products.

There's been a flurry of new books posted on Amazon recently that promise readers they can strike it rich selling medical supplies, or by dropshipping products from wholesalers, or worse yet—they suggest you can make a huge profit by locating items on Amazon and reselling them on eBay. The "prophets" or "gurus" call this arbitrage, but it's more like an elaborate Ponzi scheme. It might work, but more likely, it's going to tarnish your seller reputation.

Here's why.

When you drop ship an item or engage in Amazon—eBay arbitrage, you are relying on someone else to fulfill your orders. If they slip up, ship late, enclose the wrong invoice, or mess up something else—it's all on you. Your buyer doesn't give a damn who screwed up his order. He's going to blame you. He's going to ding your feedback rating.

Why risk it?

Some of the other books written about selling on eBay suggest you can make a killing selling Mento's tins, popsicle sticks, or the gray paper tubes inside toilet paper rolls.

No one who buys that book is going to make money selling that crap, except maybe the guy who sold it last year, and the author who wrote the book.

eBay is a dynamic marketplace. Some staples sell well every day: laptops, iPhones, top release DVDs. All these items are big money makers, but not for you or me. They're for the big players who've got a lot of money to toss around.

Smaller players like you and I survive, and thrive, on the fringe.

Let me explain.

EcommerceBytes blog ran a post a while back that featured Scott Wingo of Channel Advisor. His thoughts were eBay's holiday growth, and future growth focused more on big sellers, not small sellers - like you and me.

Most recently, Shana Champion published an article in The eBay Community blog that suggested vendors should concentrate on selling commodity products, and forget about hawking one-of-a-kind items, collectibles, and such. Her thought was commodity products offer a "more sustainable business model," because you "only have to list items once," so it's quicker and easier to sell them.

It sounds good!

But, for most sellers, it's a terrible idea.

Buying products wholesale opens up a whole new can of worms that most sellers aren't prepared to handle.

Unless you can find something unique that no one else is selling, you're not going to make any money.

The natural course on eBay is to win market share by lowering prices, and that's going to create a downward spiral in pricing on anything you try to sell.

It's not pretty.

When that happens, no one makes money. Prices go lower and lower, as everyone tries to ditch a product, and "get out" with whatever money they can salvage. The result is many products end up selling below their wholesale cost.

Enough said!

That doesn't mean you should throw your hands in the air and give up. It means you've got to play smart. You've got to know your market. You need to pick items that sell. And sell at a high enough margin to make you a decent profit.

You need to know how to market yourself and keep customers coming back to you to buy more stuff. You also need to understand how to write an effective sales listing, how to keep your eBay listing fees down, and how to ship your items safe, smart, and for the least cost.

What's that?

You think this sounds a lot like **eBay Business 101**.

It is.

If you want to make money selling on eBay, you need to think like a businessperson. I don't care if you're bagging up cow patties and selling them as new age fertilizer, or Aunt Martha's fudge square cookies.

You need to have a plan.

You need to word your item description clearly and concisely and say what you mean.

Picture this.

I'm a salesman at **Phones Are Us**.

A customer comes in, slams his phone down on the counter, and starts going off on me. "Man, this phone ain't any good. My video of my girlfriend and me is eleven marshmallow bytes long, and my phone says I need more jiggabytes of data to upload my thingee. What's up with that?"

I'm not sure whether to bust out laughing or try and explain to this guy that he's got it all wrong. He's talking pure gibberish.

A lot of eBay sellers write their listings the way this guy talks. They litter them with technical jargon, misspellings, or poorly picked words.

The way you word your listing needs to be appropriate to what you're selling. Don't talk tech if you're selling a flash drive.

Potential buyers don't want a whole bunch of tech talk or specifications. They want to know what's in it for them. How is your product going to help them solve their problems? Is it easy to use, or is there a complicated set-up procedure that will take them forever to learn?

If you're selling a memory stick with 32 gigabytes, say. "This memory stick has 32 gigabytes of data so that it will hold all your pictures, videos, and data. There's no need to worry about missing a picture when you use this product. And, getting started is as easy as plugging it in."

Make it simple.

Tell buyers what you're selling, how it will help them, and why they should buy from you rather than from the next listing.

When you provide buyers with the information, they need it reassures them. It helps them feel they're making the right decision by purchasing your flash drive.

These are just a few of the topics we're going to cover in **eBay 2020**.

Why listen to me?

Hey there, Nick Vulich, here.

If you're like me, I'm sure you're probably a little skeptical about taking advice from someone without knowing a bit about them first.

I've been selling on eBay since 1999. Most of my online customers know me as history-bytes. I've also operated as *It's Old News*, Back Door Video, and Sports Card One.

I've sold more than 40,000 items for a total of $500,000 over the past fifteen years, and that's just on my history-bytes id. I've taken a break from selling on eBay and Amazon to concentrate on my writing and coaching, but I keep my hat in the game—constantly keeping in touch with sellers, and reading the latest reports on e-commerce.

I've been an eBay Power Seller, or Top-Rated Seller, for most of the past fifteen years, which means I've paid my dues and met eBay's rigid sales and customer satisfaction goals.

eBay 2020 is the thirteenth book I have written about how to sell on eBay. The first two, *Freaking Idiots Guide to Selling on eBay*, and *eBay Unleashed* are aimed more towards how to get started selling on eBay. *eBay Subject Matter Expert* suggests a different approach to selling on eBay – building a platform where customers recognize you as an expert in your niche and buy from you because of your knowledge in that field. *Sell It Online* gives a brief overview of how to sell on eBay, Amazon, Etsy, and Fiver. *How to Make Money Selling Old Books & Magazines on eBay* talks specifically about what I know best, how to sell books and periodicals on eBay. *eBay Bookkeeping Made Easy* helps sellers understand how to keep track of the money they are making, and how to take advantage of the tax code to make even more money. *eBay Shipping Simplified* helps sellers determine the best way to ship their items, and how to use eBay's shipping tools to make the task easier. It also has a primer on international shipping and using third party shipping providers such as Stamps.com and Endicia.

eBay 2015 (also known as *eBay Selling Advanced*) is my longest book to date and encapsulates everything sellers need to know to start and grow their eBay business. *eBay 2016* (also known as *eBay Business Expert*) takes a different approach—showing sellers how to increase sales by employing well thought out social media marketing campaigns using Facebook, Twitter, Pinterest, and other sites. It also takes a close look at blogging for online sellers and how to fund special projects using Kickstarter.

This book is a serious rewrite of the eBay portion of my book—*Sell It Online*. Pretty much everything has been rewritten and revised with up-to-date information. At the back of this book, you will find five outtakes from some of my previous books—I guess you could call them my greatest hits. They contain information you can use to grow your eBay business. It should help tie up all the loose ends so that you can sell more successfully on eBay.

Let's get started.

So How Do You Get Started Selling on eBay?

Getting started selling on eBay is about as easy as it gets. The folks at eBay offer a lot of great tutorials, and the sell your item form walks you through a lot of the information you need along the way.

To begin selling, you're going to need to register for an eBay and PayPal account, if you don't already have them.

eBay offers casual sellers fifty free auction listings every month. I would suggest you use them to list a few items. This way, you can test the waters to make sure you're comfortable selling on eBay before you invest a lot of time, or money, into something you might not like.

Selling on eBay can be a lot of fun, but it's not for the feint-of-heart, or someone looking to score a quick profit. Test the waters before you jump in with both guns blazing.

Be a buyer first, then become a seller

If you've never purchased anything on eBay, it's going to be hard for you to be a good seller.

The reason I say this is it's a lot easier to be a good seller once you understand why and how people buy stuff on eBay.

People shop on eBay for many different reasons. Some people make purchases on eBay because they're looking for items on the cheap. They want to wear designer clothes, but they can't afford to buy them new.

Collectors scour the eBay listings every day looking for that rare missing piece they want to add to their collection. These are the people sellers love to have bid on their auctions because they get lost in their desire to have the item and end up fueling a bidding frenzy.

Other people shop on eBay because they don't like to go to stores. They're tired of pushy salespeople, crowded parking lots, and stores that run out of stock on the items they want. Shopping on eBay saves these people time and frustration. It's like picking your groceries up at WalMart to beat the rush and standing in line. Buying on eBay is convenient.

Some people savor the excitement. For them buying on eBay is a lot like spending a day at the race track. They like to bid on items and win things at auction. It's the rush of excitement, and the thrill of winning these people are after.

You need to buy a few things first and experience some of these emotions before you start to sell on eBay. In the long run, it will help you to understand better what your buyers want, and why they are buying from you.

Another reason you need to be a buyer first is you need to rack up some good feedback before you start selling.

One of the great things about eBay is buyers and sellers can rate each transaction they participate in, and grade each other on a scale of from one to five. eBayers strive for five-star feedback because it offers social proof that they are a reliable seller who delivers a great buying experience.

People are going to be leery of buying from you if you hang out your shingle and start trying to sell with a big old zero for your feedback rating. That zero is going to make potential buyers scream out. "Danger, Will Robinson! Danger!" because you are an unknown quantity. This is especially true if you're selling higher-priced items or items where there are lots of sellers with awesome feedback offering similar stuff.

The easiest way around this is to buy a few things. Pay quickly, leave great feedback for the seller, and wait to receive feedback for your purchases.

My suggestion is to buy ten or fifteen small items over a week. Once you have ten five-star feedback ratings under your belt, it's time to get started selling.

What should you sell?

Deciding what to sell is one of the toughest decisions most new sellers face. It doesn't have to be.

Chances are you have great things all around you—things that have been collecting dust for a long time on the shelves in your attic, garage, or basement.

Walk around your house for a few minutes. Gather up five or ten items and get ready to watch the magic begin.

Listing items you already own is an excellent way to de-clutter and get rid of all the stuff you've meant to throw away or sell at a yard sale over the years.

Do you have an old VCR that still works, but you never use anymore? Bundle it up with a stack of movies, and it could be a great seller. Many people still swear by VCR's—especially the older ones, because the newer ones no longer have built-in tuners. Be sure to tell people if your VCR has a tuner. You could get more money from it.

I have a junk drawer that has five or six old cell phones in it. Some of them work. Some of them don't. I bet I could bundle them up for a quick sale on eBay. What about your DVD collection? Have you stopped watching your DVD's because it's more convenient to watch movies on demand from your cable and satellite provider, or Netflix? Bundle them up, and you could score some quick cash on eBay.

Old video games are another quick seller on eBay. If your kids are anything like mine, they've gone through five or six video game systems over the last several years, and now the old ones are stacked in the corners of their room or your living room. Sell those old game consoles on eBay and free-up some space.

Is your closet full of clothes you no longer wear? How about the kids? Younger kids outgrow their clothes every six months, or even sooner. There is a huge market on eBay for used clothing, especially name brands or designer brands for adults or kids.

Are you beginning to understand? You probably have at least fifty to one hundred items sitting around the house that buyers on eBay would love to own.

Take advantage of this opportunity to jump in and test the waters to see if selling on eBay is right for you.

Different ways to sell on eBay

There are several ways to sell your items on eBay. Over time you will want to add them all to your toolbox.

Auctions

Auctions are what made eBay famous. Many listings start for as little as a penny. The final selling price is determined by what people are willing to pay. With a bit of luck and a good description, that one-cent starting price can turn into fifty, even one hundred dollars or more—if you can catch a wave of bidders.

Fixed Price

Fixed price listings are just like shopping at Walmart or Target. Sellers list their items for sale. If a buyer wants the article, they can purchase it at the offered price.

Classified

Classified listings are a whole different animal altogether. They are used more by businesses than by everyday sellers. An example would be if you are trying to sell a home or business. The idea behind a classified listing is to capture leads and get people to call or email you. When they use an auction or fixed price listing, sellers aren't allowed to include contact information—such as a personal email address or a phone number. Classified listings provide a workaround for this.

Other types of businesses that use classified listings are website designers, and people selling specialty advertising, such as custom imprinted shirts and pens.

eBay has several add-ons that allow sellers to turbocharge their fixed price and auction listings.

Buy-it-now

Buy-it-now is an option eBayers can add to items they are selling at auction. It lets buyers purchase an item immediately, rather than waiting for the auction to end.

eBay requires the buy-it-now price to be at least 30% more than the starting price. So, if you start your item at $10.00, your buy-it-now price should be at least $13.00. My suggestion is 30% is not a big enough jump.

When I run auctions with a buy-it-now, I shoot for the moon. If I start my item at $9.99, I set my buy-it-now price at $25.99. In one out of ten auctions that close successfully, I get the $25.99. If I'm selling a book, I have a good feeling about it; sometimes I'll go crazy and set my buy-it-now price at $99.99, $179.99, or $249.99.

The cool thing is I can often sell my item for that outrageous number because I take the time to craft a winning description that builds value for my book. I get that figure even when other sellers are offering the same book with a $10.00 or $20.00 buy-it-now price.

Don't let yourself get suckered into playing the price game, and always offering the lowest price. It's all about how you position yourself and the items you sell.

Best Offer

Best offer is an option sellers can add to their fixed-price listings. Best offer lets sellers be flexible on their asking price.

Here's how it works.

The buyer sets the price he wants for his item, then allows sellers to send him the best offer. Pricing can be a little tricky when you do this because the offers you get will be all over the board.

What I've found is you tend to get three types of offers:

- They lowball you at $5.00 or $10.00, no matter what your asking price is.
- They offer you half of your asking price.
- They ask for a few bucks off to cover the cost of shipping.

So how do you handle best offers?

I like to put my listings on auto-pilot whenever possible. That keeps eBay from sending me a bunch of low-ball offers. When you select best offer, eBay lets you set two options:

- Decline all prices below a certain number

- Accept all offers above a certain amount. By doing this, you only need to deal with the offers where you still have a chance to make money.

Sometimes, I'll say what the hell! And accept the offer—even though it's a little less than I expected. Most times I try to deal with the person making the offer to see if I can get them to bump their price up a notch or two.

The way I do this is to send them a counteroffer, along with a short note. "Sorry, the best I can do is $15.00 plus shipping. It really is a nice item in excellent condition." Doing this throws the ball back into the buyer's court. They can decline my offer, or send back a counter offer.

You're going to end up closing the sale about fifty percent of the time when you send a counteroffer, so you need to decide whether to take the first offer or to shoot for a better deal.

Reserve Price

Another option is to set a **reserve price** when you are selling with the auction format. Unless you're selling an extremely valuable or one of a kind item, a reserve price is probably not the best option. A reserve price is guaranteed to make buyers think your stuff is over-priced. A better strategy is to set a starting price you can live with and take your chances. You've got to be fearless. If you get down to the last ten minutes and things aren't looking good, the natural response is to pull the plug and yank the listing, but that isn't always the best option. Often, the most heated bidding action takes place in the last five or ten minutes. Check how many people are watching your listing before you make any moves you may later regret.

Fees – How much does it cost to sell on eBay

Costs add up quickly when you sell on eBay. I've had a lot of months where eBay's take from my earnings has been as high as $2,000.

There are two types of eBay sellers. Those with eBay stores, and those without eBay stores.

Store sellers pay a basic fee every month. In return, eBay provides them with a location to host their items and a set number of free listings.

There are additional fees for listing upgrades, such as buy-it-now, reserve auctions, and picture packs. For a complete breakdown of eBay fees, search for seller fees on eBay.

Selling on eBay is easy once you understand the rules of the game.

To consistently make sales on eBay, you need to do four things well:

- Craft a great title.
- Write a benefit's driven description.
- Include close-up pictures.
- Get the price right.

Title

Your title is the number one sales tool available to you on eBay. It's how people find what you're selling.

eBay gives you eighty characters to broadcast your message, so you need to get it right. The best strategy is to pack your title with keywords that help potential buyers find your item.

Don't worry about how your title reads.

It doesn't have to make any sense. What it needs to do is include all the possible combinations someone may use to search for your item—brand, name, model number, version, year made, color, accessories included, new/used, warranty, and misspellings if there are any common ones.

Here are a few great titles for iPads currently listed on eBay:

- Apple iPad 3rd Generation 16 GB Wi-Fi + Unlocked (Verizon) 9.7" – Black
- Brand New Apple iPad 3rd Generation 64 GB White Wifi + 4G (AT & T) 9.7" White (MD371LL/A)
- Apple iPad 3rd Generation 16 GB Wi-Fi Cracked Screen, Works
- Apple iPad 3rd Generation 16 GB Wi-Fi MC705LL/A Fully Functional Cracked Screen

Description

A good description tells buyers everything they need to know about the item.

It should tell potential buyers who made it, what the model number is, the color, the size, and what condition it's in. Is it new? Is it new in the box with tags? Is it gently used, but in like-new condition?

Put yourself in the buyer's shoes for a moment. What would you need to know if you wanted to buy your item? If you are unsure about what details to include, check what other sellers say about similar things. Make a few notes, and include some of the better information in your description.

Be upfront about condition related issues. Is there a scratch? Is there a chip in the paint? Are there some light grass stains on the knees of those jeans?

Be your own worst critic? Point out all the flaws in the items you're selling. Better people should learn about any problems with your item before they buy it than after it arrives on their doorstep. The last thing you want is negative feedback, or to have to pay return shipping because you didn't provide an accurate description.

Here are some great descriptions to give you an idea of what you should say:

1954 was the first year when Hank, featured in the Topps #128 Hank Aaron baseball card, played as an outfielder for the Milwaukee Braves. A smart photograph of Hank Aaron with his full name and autograph is featured on the front of this 1954 card. The back of this Hank Aaron baseball card supplies you with all his vital information and other Major League records. Due to his immense popularity, this Hank Aaron baseball card is nearing the top of the record books in baseball history. Fun and fantastic, the Topps #128 also makes a perfect gift for the baseball fan.

You are bidding on an original 1958 Topps Mickey Mantle card #150. Look at the quality of this card, NICE! It is 100% authentic and unaltered—guaranteed! This card has absolutely no creases, the corners have a nice form with tip touches, the centering is superb, has perfect clear imagery, has deep vibrant colors, has shiny original gloss, is clean, and the card has awesome eye appeal. There are no pinholes, markings, paper loss, stains, or any other damage of that kind. This is a beautiful card from one of the game's greatest players. It's a keeper. The card shown is the one you will receive. Please check out the images. The quality of the card will speak for itself.

They're great descriptions. They tell a good story. What sets them apart, even more, is many of the sellers in the sports card category only post a picture of the front and back of the card, with no description.

These guys make more sales because they take the time to craft killer descriptions.

Pictures

Pictures sell more stuff. Make no mistake about it, very few people are going to buy your stuff if you don't include at least one image. More pictures are always better.

Ask yourself this. Would you shell out $400 for a used laptop if you couldn't see a picture of it first? Probably not.

Suppose I'm selling a rare Hummel figurine and my description says it's in mint condition except for a small chip at the bottom of one leg. What would you think if I only showed you one picture of the entire figurine? You'd probably have some lingering doubts about that chip, wouldn't you? As a seller, I could have quickly closed the deal by including several close-up pictures of the chipped area. Several well shot, close-up photos would make it easy to determine whether the chip is a deal-breaker or not.

You need to take a good look at every item you sell. Put yourself in the buyer's shoes. What parts of the article would you need to see to decide if you want to buy that item? For a baseball card, you need to see the front and back of the card. If you're buying a laptop, you'd probably want to see a picture of it with the Windows logo displayed on the screen as proof that it works. You'd also want to see a photo showing any accessories included with the laptop—cords, case, manuals, discs, and anything other goodies.

If you sell clothes, examine how some of the most successful sellers do it. They model their outfits on male and female manikins because it gives potential buyers a better frame of reference for what they're buying rather than just looking at a flat picture of a blouse or pair of jeans. They include close-up images of designs and any flaws they described.

Price

Price is important when you sell on eBay, but it's just one piece of the puzzle. If you've taken the time to write an amazing title, craft a description that sells, and include plenty of close-up pictures, you're entitled to ask for a premium price.

Too many sellers let themselves get caught up playing the price game. They get stuck with the mentality that people shop based on price—exclusively.

Most buyers are willing to pay a little more if you give them a reason.

Think about the last time you shopped one of the big-box stores for a large screen TV. You probably went to the warehouse store because the ad featured a 42" TV for $349.00. The salesman likely asked you a few questions before he showed you that one. On the way to it, he stopped at a 50" Smart TV so he could show you how easily it can hook up to the Internet through your wifi connection. He might have mentioned how easy that makes it to watch movies on Netflix and Hulu. Did he hand your kids a pair of 3D glasses so they could get a good look at the dinosaur popping out of the picture?

What happened next?

Odds are you bought the $999 Smart TV, or the more expensive 3D TV because it had all those great features you hadn't considered.

eBay buyers aren't any different than shoppers at a big-box store. They might have every intention of grabbing the least expensive book or pair of jeans when they start shopping, but if you give them a compelling reason to spend a little more, they will most likely open up their wallets and pay a bit more than they planned.

My point is: If you're happy getting the same price everyone else is, go ahead and use the same lame-ass description everyone else is using. If you want the big bucks, think of each of your listings as a work of art. Craft a compelling story that will make people beg you to take their money.

Now, I'm going to share a few secrets with you to help you step your game up a bit, so you can save time and make more money selling on eBay.

Brand your eBay store.

eBay stores level the playing field and make it easier for you to compete with the big guys. They let you look like a big business, even if you're a one-man shop working part-time from your kitchen table.

A custom storefront lets you offer your customers a unique shopping experience.

eBay sellers can create custom pages to share information and product details with their clients. The problem is very few eBayers use them.

That's a big mistake!

Used correctly, custom pages can improve your customer's shopping experience and your sales. Here are a few ideas based on how I've seen eBay sellers use their custom pages:

- Include a sizing chart for clothing that explains how customers should take measurements.
- Show the measurements associated with each size for men's, women's, and children's clothing.
- Explain how your items are packaged and shipped (this is especially important if you have an upcharge for shipping because of the extra care you take in packaging items).
- Tips on how to take care of the items you are selling.
- If you sell custom items, like imprinted clothing, pens, or mugs, explain what information you need from customers to make the project happen.
- Tell your story. What drove you to get into this business? What makes your business unique? Why should customers buy from you rather than one of your competitors?
- If you sell graded sports memorabilia, explain what grading is, and the different grading services you use.
- If you sell collectibles, you can tell how you grade your products.

- Design custom landing pages for different groups of your products.

Automate your shipping.

eBay and PayPal have some useful shipping tools integrated into them, but once you start selling more items, or if you are selling on multiple platforms, you're going to want a more advanced tool.

Stamps.com is run by the United States Post Office and can help sellers mail their products more efficiently. Stamps.com users can easily import buyer information from eBay, Amazon, Etsy, and other marketplaces, then print shipping labels on their home computers.

The reason I use Stamps.com is I can ship first class international packages without having to go to the post office. If you use the tools available in eBay, PayPal, and Amazon, the only international shipping options available to you are Priority International and Express International.

Accept returns

If you want to play with the big boys, you need to act like them. No one likes returns, but everyone wants to make more sales. Accepting returns is the best way to encourage more people to buy from you.

When I first started ramping up my sales on eBay, I offered "a 100% Money Back Guarantee. No questions asked."

Over the last fourteen years, I've had less than ten returns. Probably fifty people have requested to return something, but after I let them know it wasn't a problem and I'd be happy to take their item back, most of them decided they would rather keep it.

Offer a return policy and see how it affects your business. If it doesn't work out, you can always change your policies down the road.

Create Special Sales

Use *Mark Down Manager* to create limited-time sales for your customers, or to sell slow-moving inventory. *Mark Down Manager* is a tool available to eBay store owners. You can access it in the *Marketing Tools* section of *Selling Manager*.

Mark Down Manager lets you selectively discount store items. You can provide a discount (so many dollars off), or entice customers to purchase additional items (buy three, get one free). Try one method one week, and a different one the next week. I try to run a different sale every week because each time you run a new sale, eBay emails your customers to let them know about your promotion. They give you one more chance to make the sale.

Promotions aren't a sure thing. Sometimes they work better than others, but it's worth a shot if you need to raise some extra cash fast.

Be open to new ideas

Your customer's wants and needs change over time. Your eBay business needs to be flexible so you can change with them.

Keep tabs on your competition. Watch what your target market is doing.

Hang out where your customers do online and offline. Listen to what they are saying. Are their favorite websites featuring new products? Pay attention to the trends you see happening and cater to them. Take a few baby steps now and again. Try selling some new items. Some of them will work out. Some of them won't. Over time, you will wind up carrying more products your customers want, need, and are willing to spend their money on.

Don't be afraid to change directions

If you've given it your best shot, and it's not working, don't be afraid to change directions. Maybe you need to reinvent the way you're branding yourself, or presenting your product. Perhaps you need to kiss the old product line goodbye and reinvent yourself with a whole new product line.

There's no shame in reinventing your business. Most people reinvent their careers three to five times throughout their work life. Why should your eBay business be any different?

Send Offers to Your Buyers

I have to admit, I was on the line when eBay added this feature, but it works. I sell about 20 percent of the offers I send. I could probably jump that to 40 or 50 percent if I offered deeper discounts.

If you haven't tried sending your customers offers yet, go to my eBay and select <send offers—eligible>. It's a list of people who are watching your stuff. Every day, eBay lets you send offers targeted buyers who are watching that item. I'm not sure how they decide which ones are eligible. All I know is it works, especially if you can reel in a buyer who's watching five or ten items.

The only caveat is that you can only send one offer, so you've got to submit your best offer upfront. I usually discount my stuff 20 to 25 percent. Play around with your items, and you'll find out what works best for you.

How to list your first item on eBay

Now it's time for a quick walkthrough about how to sell on eBay.

The easiest way to start a listing is to search for the item you want to sell. Underneath the gallery pictures at the top of the listing page, you will see -

$ **Have one to sell?** Sell it yourself

Click where it says, "Sell it yourself." The sell your item form walks you through the process and will help you list your first item in no time.

Category

Make sure you choose the correct category for what you want to sell. Research shows 80% of buyers search by the item name, but 20% of people browse categories to discover new articles when they are shopping. If you list your stuff in the wrong category, you're going to miss the opportunity to sell to these people.

Title

You get eighty characters to describe your item. Be sure you make it keyword-rich, and loaded with terms buyers will use to search for your item.

Subtitle

Subtitle is an optional feature and costs from .50 to $1.50 depending on the style of listing you are using. If you're listing a unique or a high dollar value item, using a subtitle may be a good choice. Keep in mind people can't search by the terms you include in your subtitle. Its purpose is to give buyers a little extra information so they can decide whether to click on your listing or not.

Subtitle does cost extra, so only use it when you think it can help sell your item. Another thing to keep in mind when you use a subtitle, or any other listing enhancements, is when you relist your item, you're going to pay that extra fee again and again.

Be sure to keep track when you use listing enhancements, and remove them before you relist your item if you no longer want to use them.

Condition description

Condition description lets you make a quick comment about any issues relating to your item. What I like about it is it your comments show up right at the top of your listing. When you add comments here, tell people all the faults your item has, but be sure to word it, so you minimize your product's defects.

If you're selling a rare book, you could word it like this. "This book has a few small pencil marks scattered throughout the first three chapters, but none of them interfere with reading the text. Other than this, the book is in very nice condition." Notice what I did. I told potential buyers the book had some defects (pencil marks), but otherwise, it was "very nice." When you word your description this way, it creates the perception that the problem you listed isn't that bad.

Item Specifics

Item specifics change based on the item you are selling. Not all categories require you to fill these out, but if you do, they can help you come up higher in search when people filter their search by size, color, etc.

Pictures

eBay lets you add up to twelve free pictures with each listing. Photos are required to be:

- At least 500 pixels on the longest edge. eBay recommends 1600 pixels for the best picture quality.
- Borders are not allowed around pictures.
- Sellers cannot add any text or artwork to their photos
- At least one photo must be uploaded for every listing, even if you sell using eBay's catalog.

I used to scan all my pictures, then run them through Adobe Lightroom to size them correctly, but the new digital cameras are so good, I just snap a few pictures and upload them. You can do any necessary editing in eBay's photo tool.

Description

You can enter your item description in plain text or HTML. HTML can spruce up an auction listing template or enhance the listing in some other way.

If you use a template, you should paste it into this box, and make whatever changes you need to customize it for each listing.

Themes

Themes are a form of template. eBay charges ten cents for each listing that use them. My advice is to take a pass on themes. If you want to use a template to spruce up, your listings sign up for a service like Auctiva or Ink Frog. They host your pictures and include a wide selection of free templates.

Choose how you'd like to sell your item

Do you want to sell your item at auction or fixed price?

Both methods have their place. When they first got started, eBay focused on auction-style listings. Over the last five years, most of the action has shifted to fixed-price listings, where there is no bidding. People just click on the item and purchase it.

Everyone has their preference on which listing format works best. Much of it comes down to what you're selling.

If you're listing a unique item or something where the selling price is not well known, or frequently fluctuates, such as hot concert tickets or collectibles, the auction format should bring you a better price.

For commodity items or items that sell in a close price range, fixed priced listings are a better choice.

If you have an item that is selling well, you may want to vary the length of your listings. Try one day, three days, five days, seven days, and thirty-day listings. Include buy-it-now on all your auction listings, and use a higher price for your fixed price listings. This strategy will maximize your sales and the final amount you receive for them.

If you're selling in the auction format, enter your starting price. If you want to include a buy-it-now price, list it in the appropriate box. Below that enter how many items you are selling. In the radio box for the duration, select how long you want the listing to run.

Schedule start time allows you to decide what time your item should start selling. eBay charges an extra ten cents to use this feature. My thought is there are plenty of buyers out there for your item whenever you decide to start and end it. Some people swear between 5:00 and 8:00 pm is the best time to end your listings, other people insist Sunday is the best day. It's your dime - pick a strategy you like and run with it.

eBay Giving Works

When you sell with Giving Works, you can donate anywhere from 10% to 100% of the selling price to your favorite charity. When your item sells, eBay will credit you back a portion of the selling fees.

The best part about selling with eBay Giving Works is they have thousands of local charities signed up. Chances are you can quickly discover ten or twenty local charities to support in your neck of the woods.

Charity listings draw more page views. In my experience, I often receive two to three times as many page views when I sell for a cause.

Getting Paid

PayPal is eBay's preferred payment method. It's linked to eBay, and most people are comfortable using PayPal. Another thing to remember is your customer doesn't have to have a PayPal account to pay with PayPal. They can enter their bank or credit card info into the secure form and make their payment without ever signing up for PayPal.

eBay is currently converting its platform over to their managed payments systems. Just be aware that change is coming.

Shipping details

There are two sections you need to work with here. One is for domestic shipping (in the country you are in), and the other is international shipping (to foreign countries).

You have four shipping methods to choose from:

- **Flat rate shipping** means you charge the same shipping rate to everyone regardless of location. If you have a small item, such as a postcard or a book, you can tell everyone you will ship it for a certain amount. Sometimes it will cost you a little more, sometimes a little less. The good thing is flat rate shipping is easy to understand. If you say $4.00, everyone pays $4.00 for that item to be shipped.

- **Calculated shipping** means you input the weight of your item into the shipping details; then, eBay automatically calculates the shipping cost to each buyer's location. The shipping fees your buyer pays depend upon how much it costs to ship the item to them. When eBay displays the shipping amount, they figure it based upon what it would be for that particular buyer. It's beneficial if you live closer to a buyer because your shipping could be less expensive than that offered by sellers who live further away.

- **Freight** is calculated for shipments over 150 pounds. Freight shipping is for larger and heavier items that need to ship by an over-the-road truck line.

- **Local pickup** means the buyer can pick the purchase up at the seller's location. Select this option when the stuff you're selling is very fragile or is bulky and hard to pack. I've seen buyers use it with furniture, exercise equipment, or when they are selling collections of books. Because the items are large and difficult to pack, sellers often don't want to go to the trouble and expense of doing it, so they limit shipping to local pickup only.

International shipping

Many sellers are afraid to offer international shipping because they're not sure how it works. The truth is international shipping isn't any harder than shipping in your home country. The major difference is you need to include a custom label with most international shipments, which lists the contents of the package and its value.

Your local post office can walk you through it the first few times, or if you are printing shipping labels online, the program will walk you through all the steps.

One thing I would suggest with international shipments is to set delivery expectations for your customers. When you mail a package, send a quick email to the recipient to tell them their shipment is on the way. You may want to say something like this in the email, "Thank you for your order. I mailed your package today. International delivery time runs two to three weeks, but can take as many as six to eight weeks depending on customs and local post offices." Doing this will save you a lot of customer service emails with clients who don't receive their packages the next week.

eBay also has something called the Global Shipping Program. It makes shipping items internationally as easy as mailing within your home country. To opt in to the program, you select the Global Shipping Program under the international shipping options when you're listing your item. When an item sells internationally, eBay notifies you to send it to one of their shipping partners within the United States. When the package reaches the shipping center, your responsibility is over. The shipping center repackages the item, fills out customs forms, and sends it on its way.

Once you begin to make more international sales, you might want to opt-out of eBay's Global Shipping Program. It's convenient, but the high prices they charge scare the bejeesus out of buyers. Over time, eBay's Global Shipping Program is going to cost you at least 50 percent of your international sales.

Other things you'd like buyers to know

The first item here allows you to set bidder requirements, such as not allowing bidders with two or more recent non-paying bidder strikes to bid on your auctions.

If you have a sales tax permit, select the state you want to collect sales tax in and the amount eBay should charge. If your item sells in that state, eBay will collect tax on the item for you and list it separately on the invoice for you and your buyer.

Even if you don't collect sales tax, eBay will collect it for you in more than a dozen states. It's a new law that more states are instituting to up their sales tax revenue.

Return policy

eBay doesn't require you to accept returns—yet, but I would strongly recommend doing so. It will increase your sales. If you decide to accept returns, you need to check the boxes and state how soon the buyer needs to return the item and who pays return shipping – the buyer or the seller. You should also state a return policy in the box provided. Mine is, *"Here at history-bytes we understand buying items sight unseen on the internet can be scary at times. For this reason, we offer a 100 % MONEY BACK GUARANTEE. You can return your item within 14 days for a full refund – No Questions Asked."*

The final box on this page gives you a chance to list any additional checkout instructions. Usually, all I say here is "PayPal is the only payment method we accept."

At the very bottom of the page, it shows you **your fees so far**. After this, click continue to move on to the next page.

eBay takes one more shot to sell you some of their listing enhancements, such as gallery plus, subtitle, and bold. My advice is just to say no! Unless you have something special, selecting any of these options is going to be just like throwing your money down the garbage disposal.

At the bottom of this page, it displays a summary of your fees. If everything looks okay, click on list your item, and it will go live on eBay. If you want to see how it looks first, click on preview listing, and it will generate a preview of your listing for you to review.

Selling on eBay can be easy, fun, and profitable.

Start out slow. Baby-step it. Try listing a few items you have around the house. If you decide eBay is a good match for you, uncover for a niche you can fill, and target products to it.

Build your business slowly. Test new products, discard the losers, and keep the winners. Over time you will discover you have a strong business with a steady stream of repeat buyers looking for the new products you have added.

Craft an Amazing Title

Everyone who buys something from you is going to read your title. Everyone who does and doesn't buy from you is going to read your title. Make it compelling so buyers will click on your listing. Make it so so, and they will move on to the next item.

Here's something else you need to know. Over fifty percent of the people who buy from you only look at the title and pictures in your listing. They won't read your description, your policies, or anything else. If the title and pictures look good, they will click buy—even if they're not sure about what they're buying.

That could mean trouble down the line.

But for now, let's concentrate on how to create a clickable title. A title that answers all of a buyer's questions, and makes them want to learn more.

As I said earlier, your title doesn't need to be a literary masterpiece. It doesn't even have to make sense. Its sole purpose is to grab a potential buyer's attention and get them to click on your listing.

eBay gives you eighty characters to describe your item. Your goal is to cram every last detail and keyword you can into those eighty characters.

The first thing to know is your title is how people are going to find the item you're selling on eBay. eBay uses the words in your title to determine who will see your article. Because of this, it's important to use every possible word or combination of words someone might search by in the title.

Your title doesn't have to read well or even make sense to be effective. It just needs to contain as many keywords as possible to maximize the chances it will be displayed when someone searches for a similar item.

Unfortunately, many people waste this valuable space, trying to get cutesy or to write a sentence that makes sense. The fact is no one is going to search for "very nice," "awesome," "great," or "one-of-a-kind." You would be much better off giving a professional descriptor like "near-mint" or "MS65," because these are terms collectors are looking for.

Here are some tips for writing better titles:

- **Include as many keywords as possible**. You've got eighty characters. Use as many of them as you can in each of your titles. Don't worry that your title doesn't make sense. Just be sure to include all of the keywords you think someone would use to describe the item you are selling.

- **Double Check Your Spelling**. To get found by the maximum number of people, spell everything correctly. If you're in doubt, use spell check.
- **Avoid using adjectives and descriptive phrases**. Save all of the adjectives and descriptive phrases for your item description. No one searches for "very nice" – "LQQK" – or "WoW!"
- **Avoid excess capitalization**. No one likes it when you shout or try too hard to sell them. If you absolutely must use all capitalization, only do it to one word, not your entire title.
- **Use the correct terms**. If you are unfamiliar with the item you're selling, take a moment to Google it. One thing I've discovered over the years is people love to criticize you when you misspell a word, put an item in the wrong category, or misdescribe it. Sometimes it feels like they're crawling out of the woodwork and gunning for you.
- **Include common misspellings**. If the item you're selling is frequently misspelled on eBay, include the misspellings in your title if you have room.
- **Don't use abbreviations**. Abbreviations confuse customers. If there is any doubt, spell it out. If you don't have room in your title for the word you want to use, chose another word with a similar meaning. The exception here would be commonly accepted abbreviations on eBay. NWT – New with tags, NIB – New in the box, BNWT – Brand new with tags, FS – Factory sealed.

With all that said, one of the hardest things for many sellers to do is decide which keywords to put in your title.

Perhaps the easiest way to determine which keywords to include in your title is to look at other auctions for similar items. How do they describe the item? What keywords do they use? What words do you see show up in other auctions?

After you've made the above list, take a minute to put yourself in the buyer's shoes. What words would you use to describe the item you're selling? Those are the keywords you want to include in your title.

Create an Amazing Description

It never ceases to amaze me when I see a high-end listing with a one-line description.

WTF!

Other than your title and pictures, your description is the best tool you have to nail it and close the sale. Don't get lazy now! Ask yourself, what's it going to take to move someone from maybe—to, "Hell Yeah!"

Here's what I mean.

The following description accompanied a book currently listed for sale on eBay with an asking price of $349.99. It reads:

Samuel Brown. An Authentic History of the Second War for Independence. (Auburn, 1815) Vol .1.
6 5/8 inch high

Not much to go on is there?

The seller posted six high-resolution photos that give you a good idea of the condition. From what I can see, the cover is in good shape with some minor chipping. I don't see much foxing or yellowing on the pages, but I can only see four of them, so I can't be sure. And, what about the binding? Is it tight? Are the pages about ready to bust loose from the seams? And does anyone know? Is it a first or second edition?

Face it; there are a lot of unanswered questions here.

I love old books, especially from the period covering the Revolutionary War to the Civil War, but I would have to pass on this one. I can't help asking myself what issues is the seller hiding from me?

It's a shame really, because it's an important early work on the War of 1812, and the price is right on the money.

The seller could have turned the whole thing around if he'd taken time out to ask himself, what information does the buyer need to make an informed decision? Does he (or she) need to know more about the condition? The content? Or, what sellers on other sites are charging for that book?

As soon as you answer those questions, you can craft a fantastic description that tells potential buyers everything they need to know to move from maybe to yes.

Try this one on for size:

Samuel Brown. An Authentic History of the Second War for Independence. (Auburn, 1815) vol.1.

If you're interested in the War of 1812, the book is a must-have. Brown served as a private in the Ohio Militia. He fought against the Shawnee Chief Tecumseh at the Battle of Thames and pursued the British troops after the Battle of Lake Erie.

The book itself is in excellent condition. It's volume one of a two-part series and would make an excellent addition to any Military Collection. The only other copy listed online is available from Biblio for $850 (for both volumes).

The book is 6 ½ inches tall by 4 ½ inches wide. There are some mild foxing and age spots, but everything is readable. There's a faded name, penciled on the flyleaf, and some scattered pencil marks on the first few pages (see scans). From the research I've done, it's not the first edition, but it is an 1815 printing.

Do you see the difference?

This description answers the questions buyers need to know to make an informed decision. It tells you the title, publication, size, page condition, and provides a brief biography of the author. It lets you know it's rare. There's only one other copy available online, and it's selling for a hefty premium.

Could we have made it even better?

Sure. If it had been one of my listings, I would have shared several excerpts of battles and troop movements. At the very least, I would have linked to a PDF copy online at *Google Books* or the *Library of Congress*. A lot of sellers are afraid to do that because they think a buyer will read the free copy and take a pass on the listing. Not so. Collectors want to make sure of what they are buying. The best way to do that is to let them preview the content. Serious collectors will give the content a quick read through to validate it fits in with their collection. Window-shoppers will read the free content and move on to the next listing. Good riddance to them. We want buyers, not lookers.

Here's another example:

Original Niles Weekly Register published on August 6, 1814.

This issue contains a lengthy, detailed article about the Battle of Chippewa on the Niagara Frontier.

Excerpt:

"Early on July 5, British light infantry, militia, and Indians crossed the Chippawa ahead of Riall's main body and began sniping at Scott's outposts from the woods to their west. (Some of them nearly captured Scott, who was having breakfast in a farmhouse.) Brown ordered Porter's brigade and Indians to clear the woods. They did so, but they met Riall's advancing regulars and hastily retreated.

"Scott was already advancing from Street's Creek. His artillery (Captain Nathaniel Towson's company, with three 12-pounder guns) deployed on the portage road and opened fire. Riall's own guns (two light 24-pounder guns and a 5.5-inch howitzer) attempted to reply, but Towson's guns destroyed an ammunition wagon and put most of the British guns out of action.

"As the redcoats of the 1st and 100th Regiments moved forward, their own artillery had to stop firing in order to avoid hitting them. Meanwhile, the American gunners switched from firing round shot to firing canister, with lethal consequences for the British infantry. Once the opposing lines had closed to less than 100 yards apart, Scott advanced his wings, forming his brigade into a "U" shape, which

allowed his flanking units to catch Riall's advancing troops in a heavy crossfire.

"Both lines stood and fired repeated volleys; after 25 minutes of this pounding Riall, his own coat pierced by a bullet ordered a withdrawal. The 1/8th, which had been moving to the right of the other two regiments, formed line to cover their retreat. As they, in turn, fell back, three British 6-pounder guns came into action to cover their withdrawal, with two more 6-pounders firing from the entrenchments north of the Chippawa. Scott halted his brigade, although some of Porter's Iroquois pursued the British almost to the Chippawa."

Very good condition. This listing includes the complete entire original newspaper, NOT just a clipping or a page of it. We stand behind all the items we sell with a "no questions asked, money back guarantee." Every item we sell is an original newspaper printed on the date indicated at the beginning of its description. U.S. buyers pay $8 priority mail postage, which includes waterproof plastic and a heavy cardboard flat to protect your purchase from damage in the mail. Ask about international shipping rates. We do combine postage (to reduce postage costs) for multiple purchases sent in the same package.

What do you think?

It answers all the questions a buyer could have. It describes the item, provides several excerpts focused on the information collectors want, need, and are willing to pay for. And, it offers buyers a 100% Money Back Guarantee.

I know. It's a lot of work.

It takes some extra time to write a description like this, but when you do, you're more likely to command a premium price.

It's up to you.

You can do what every other seller does, and post a half-assed description, or you can put in the time it takes to craft a detailed item description guaranteed to sell your item.

I know it works.

I did it for sixteen years and built a strong business with thousands of repeat buyers.

If you want to sell on eBay or any other e-commerce website, this is the type of listing page you need to craft.

The Price is Right

Pricing is the toughest part of selling online.

It's where the rubber meets the road. It's where everything comes together

A lot of sellers start every listing at 99 cents. Others stick an outlandish price on every item they list, then slap on a buy it now. Both approaches work. Neither is a viable strategy for building a long-term business.

Pricing is one of the trickiest parts of selling on eBay or any online site, for that matter.

Price your item too high, and no one will buy it. Price your item too low, and you will be leaving profit on the table. The problem is there is no one hundred percent perfect method for pricing your item right out of the box. Pricing is more of a process, especially if you are selling multiple copies of an item.

For some items, pricing is straightforward. Commodity items people buy every day like foodstuffs, DVD's, books, electronics, all sell in a very close price range. If you step out of the accepted price range for the item, your sales will dry up quicker than you think.

Perhaps the easiest way to price your item is to search eBay to see what similar items have recently sold for. To do this, you need to use the advanced search function.

To access the Advanced Search feature, go to the top of the eBay page. To the right of the search box, you will see the word **Advanced** just after the big blue Search box. Go ahead and click on the word **Advanced**.

Type in the name or description of the item you want to search for. Scroll down a little further where it says search including and check the box by **Completed Listings**. Then click enter. It returns a list of all the ended listing for that item within the past thirty days. Items listed in green are items that have sold.

After you've done this, you will be able to see a list of all completed items on eBay. The unsold listing will appear for thirty days; sold listings will appear for ninety days. After it returns this list, you have the option to narrow your search down even further by clicking on active listings (with bids) or completed listings.

The great thing here is you can see how much items similar to yours have recently sold for on eBay.

By looking through completed listings, you can easily find the price range your item has sold in. There's no need to guess about how to price your items.

The way I use the information is to look through the titles to find items most similar to mine. Each time I click on an item, I take a few notes about any keywords the seller used in the title and item description. I also make a note of the price it sold for. If it was an auction item, I mark down the starting price. Next, I look at shipping to determine if the seller offered free shipping or the options and prices they offered for shipping.

After you do this for four or five items, you will have some great information about how to write your item description and title. It should give you an excellent idea of what you can expect your item to sell for.

At this point, we're almost ready to start pricing your item. Before you stop doing your research, I'd suggest you also click into two or three of the things that sold for the highest prices. Look over the notes you made, and see if these listings said anything different than the other ones you looked at. Specifically, did they offer a more detailed description? Did they use different keywords in the title? Did they start at a lower price? Did they use a buy-it-now?

Now you need to determine a pricing strategy.

Some people swear by starting everything at 99 cents or $9.99 and letting the market determine the price. The problem with this strategy is it only works for certain categories of items. If you're selling something that always closes in a tight price range like electronics, cell phones, iPhones, iPads, and the like, starting your item at 99 cents is going to bring in the maximum number of bidders, and will usually bring you the highest price possible for each item.

If you sell one of a kind items, collectibles, and other low demand items, starting your item at 99 cents is going to be a disaster. What's going to happen in nine out of ten cases is, if your item sells at all, it's going to sell for 99 cents, or $1.04.

A better pricing strategy with many items is to price them at the lowest price you are willing to accept and then add a buy-it-now at what you would like to get. If you are selling your item in a fixed price format, set the price somewhat higher than you hope to get, and add best offer to it.

What if you're selling something unique that isn't currently available on eBay? How do you price your item then?

If it's something you have a lot of or a lot of similar items, the best thing you can do is experiment with different price points, and determine which one sells the most items.

Let me give you an example. I sell old magazine articles, removed from bound publications. So basically, all I'm selling is a few sheets of old paper. I have a few competitors on eBay, but not many.

When I first started selling magazine articles back in 2000, I priced all of my items at $12.99, and they sold well. After six months, I increased my price to $15.99, then $19.99, and then $25.99, and sales increased each time. When I stretched it again to $27.99, sales started slowing down. As a result, I knew my optimal price range was somewhere between $19.99 and $25.99.

I found my sweet spot in auction pricing the same way. I started my items at $9.99, and many of them sold. Then I added Buy-it-Now at 15.99, $19.99, and $25.99. Once again, $25.99 provided the most conversions, so that's the formula

I went with – a $9.99 starting price, with a $25.99 Buy-it-Now.

It was a great price strategy, and it worked for years.

The next thing you know, eBay decided they wanted to be more like Amazon, and to become more of a marketplace so they could lure in the big sellers like Best Buy and Toy-R-Us.

One of the things they did was to change the emphasis to fixed-price listings rather than auctions. That sent me back to the drawing board, and once again, I reinvented my eBay business, this time focusing it on fixed price listings, with just a scattering of auction listings.

Determine What to Sell

(Most of this section was first published in my book eBay2016: Grow Your Business Using Social Media, Email Marketing, and Crowdfunding. One of the hardest things for any online seller is deciding what to sell. This section focuses on using the **Advanced Search Tool** to determine what is selling on eBay today. As a seller—it will help you make smarter choices when you source new products.)

There are a lot of books out there that tell you which items sell the best on eBay, but you don't need any of them.

eBay has the only tool you need to determine which items sell best—and it's free.

It's called the **advanced search tool**. Sellers who use it make more sales at higher prices than those who don't use it. The reason for this is simple. The **advanced search tool** shows you which items have sold in the last ninety days, how much they sold for, and—it gives you a link to the sales page so that you can check the listing out for even more pertinent clues.

"Big deal," you say. "I can find all that out by looking at current listings."

Think again.

Sellers who use the **advanced search tool** sell more stuff because it lets them know what's selling on eBay now, and how much they can expect to get when they sell something. Sellers who use the tool have insider knowledge about what's selling. Not what sold two weeks ago. Not what sold two months ago, and not what sold two years ago—but what items sold today.

Still, have some doubts?

Let's look at an example

The first thing you need to do is pick a category to sell in. To make it easier, we're going to eliminate electronics, cell phones, and name brand clothing. They're all big sellers on eBay, but unless you have an inside track to sourcing new products, it's next to impossible to make money in these hyper-competitive categories.

The iPhone 7 was one of the hottest products on the market for the 2016 Christmas season. Most retailers couldn't get their hands on any of the 128-gigabyte or 256-gigabyte models. The 32-gigabyte phones were readily available, and they sold like hotcakes.

Most of us don't have the cash it takes to make a go at selling the iPhone 7, but a quick look through eBay shows a fast-paced market in iPhone 7 accessories.

For this example, we're going to look at iPhone 7 cases to determine where the market is, so we can optimize our sales by only offering the fastest moving products. To do this, we're going to use the **advanced search tool** to narrow down our choices.

A quick search on eBay shows...

- 1,078,902 completed listings
- 259,634 sold items

This information tells us roughly 24 % of the items we list are going to sell, or conversely, 76 % of the iPhone 7 cases we list aren't going to sell.

Now let's break it down by price range.

- $ 0 to $ 10
- 205,715 sales
- 148,632 sold at auction
- 64,175 sold with Buy It Now

- $ 10 to $ 25
- 37,067 sales
- 11,190 sold at auction
- 25,750 sold with Buy It Now

- $ 25 to $50
- 13,759 sales
- 3794 sold at auction
- 10,254 sold with Buy It Now

- $50 to $100

- 1840 sales
- 685 sold at auction
- 1191 sold with Buy It Now

- $1000 to $2500
- 142 sales
- 98 sold at auction
- 46 sold with Buy It Now

A couple of interesting things pop out when you examine this list — more items sold at auction on the high and low end of the price spectrum. In the mid-range, more items sold using Buy It Now. Doing this makes it easy to pick the best listing format for your iPhone 7 cases.

The sales data can also help us select the right price range to sell in.

In this case, I chose the $25 to $50 price range. It had strong sales – 13,759 cases sold out of 28,534 listed. That's a 46 % sell-through rate; almost double that of the category-as-a-whole.

Now we can take it a step further and select the top-selling brands.

- Otterbox 3,886
- Michael Kors 1,031
- Gorilla Glass 268

Don't forget; you can do this in any category. When you do an advanced search by price point, brand, size, or some other parameter, you are more likely to choose items that are going to sell.

If you do this every time, you're going to sell more items at a higher price point.

Now that we've picked an item to sell, it's time to investigate the best way to sell it.

The Otterbox is the number one seller in the $25 to $50 price range. It comes in three varieties: Defender, Commuter, and Symmetry. Using the **advanced search tool**, we can pull up the listings that sold at higher prices to see what those sellers did differently. Sometimes, it's as simple as using more appropriate keywords in the title, more and better pictures, a stronger description, or maybe a combination of all three.

Let's look at the title first. For this example, we're going to use the Otterbox Defender.

Here are some of the keywords included in the top-selling listings:

- New
- Case and Belt Clip Holster
- iPhone 6
- Otterbox Defender Case
- Pink, Gray, Glacier, Black
- Authentic / 100 % Genuine
- Free 2-3 Day Shipping
- Case Cover Skin

Okay. We've got 80 characters to work with, so a great title would look something like this.

- Otterbox Defender Case for iPhone 6 New 100 % Authentic Black
- New Otterbox Defender Case for iPhone 6 with Belt Clip & Holster
- New Otterbox Defender Case for iPhone 6 **FREE 2 Day Shipping **

That's how you write a great selling title.

Examine the top-selling listings. Pick and choose the hottest keywords, then craft a title that jumps your listing over the competition.

Example 2

This time we're going to take an everyday item, many sellers list on eBay.

Party supplies.

Many sellers offer party packs—party hats, favors, napkins, treat bags, paper plates, and piñatas. They purchase their inventory from online suppliers, from closeouts bins at local party stores, and even from large discount stores like Walmart and Target.

The trick to making money is to know which items people are buying now.

The first step is to do a general search.

The broad term we're going to search by is party supplies. It brings up 418,033 listings. When we search for sold listings, 102,448 listings closed successfully or sold. That gives us a sell-through rate of just over 24 percent. Right off the bat that tells us this is going to be a tough category to make money in because 76 percent of all listings don't sell.

Now we can narrow it down further by seeing which items sell the best.

Sponge Bob

- 337 sales
- 96 sold at auction
- 241 sold using buy it now

Frozen

- 7629 sales
- 3596 sold at auction
- 4034 sold using buy it now

Ninja Turtles

- 642 sales
- 120 sold at auction
- 522 sold using buy it now

Cars

- 966 sales
- 317 sold at auction
- 649 sold using buy it now

Elmo

- 291 sales
- 52 sold at auction
- 239 sold using buy it now

Cat in the Hat

- 117 sales
- 25 sold at auction
- 92 sold using buy it now

Spiderman

- 691 sales
- 154 sold at auction
- 537 sold using buy it now

How to Train Your Dragon

- 117 sales
- 25 sold at auction
- 92 sold using buy it now

What pops out at me when I examine these numbers is party supplies isn't a hot selling or big money category. Many of the items listed there sell in the five to ten dollar range, with a few products stretching to twenty-five dollars or more each. *Frozen, Cars,* and *Ninja Turtles* are the hot franchises where the money is right now, so that's where you should concentrate most of your listings. Just remember, the category appears to be driven by bestselling movies, so keep an eye on what new cartoons are around the corner, and be ready to pounce on them while they're hot.

Another interesting tidbit is old standbys like *Bugs Bunny,* and the other *Looney Tunes* characters don't sell well. The same goes for the hot FOX series like the *Simpsons* and *American Dad.* Sellers should take this as a warning. Just because something is popular, doesn't mean it's going to sell well in the party supplies category. Another big-name item that surprised me was *Shrek. Shrek* is one of the biggest franchises out there, but right now, the party supply market for it is non-existent.

I wouldn't make a move in this category without researching what's selling. I wouldn't make any large quantity buys—period. The market appears quite fickle. When a new bestseller pops onto the scene, even *Frozen* could be knocked out of its top place rather quickly.

As for selling methods, buy-it-now listings outsold auction listings for every item I examined. Stick with buy-it-now listings to maximize your sales and profits. Use auctions to sell through slow-moving inventory.

I hope this helps you understand how to research what sells best.

You don't need to perform any complicated computations, but you should take more than a few minutes to explore any category you're considering. Make sure it's a profitable market segment, and that you're focusing on the bestselling portions of that market.

Even if you give in, and pick a weaker category to sell in, you should be able to scratch out a decent profit if you focus on selling the right items.

Remember, you need to do your research before you start selling in any category.

Make it Mobile Friendly

During the 2017 Christmas season, over half of the purchases made on eBay occurred on mobile devices. But, here's the funny thing. Most people didn't pay for their purchases on a mobile device. They saved the item to their cart, then moved to a laptop or desktop to make their payment.

It doesn't make sense, does it?

Unless. Maybe shoppers need to take a breather to make sure they're making the right decision? Or, perhaps they want to take one last look at what their purchase looks like on the big screen? Or, could it be shoppers are afraid to share their payment information on a mobile device?

Whatever the reason, the implications are clear.

You're not going to close every sale on the first click. Instead, many sales are going to be a two-part process. The risk is shoppers are going to abandon items in their carts.

Retailers are going to need to deploy enhanced reminder systems to counteract this trend.

At Christmas time, I searched out Iowa Hawkeye hoodies on eBay. Like many other shoppers, I added two of them to my cart but never got around to completing the purchase. Two months later, eBay is still emailing me constant reminders—return to eBay to complete your purchase—finish your transaction now and save ten percent (get FREE shipping or whatever today's current win back offer is).

Some shoppers tuck items into their carts to see what offers they will receive to complete the sale. On eBay, this strategy won't pay off because eBay doesn't control pricing—individual sellers do. But, on Amazon, it's a different story. Amazon is the seller of many of their items. If they want to make a deal and move some product, they are free to wheel and deal.

The growth of mobile shopping is no surprise. eBay, Amazon, Shopify, and other websites have been counting down to the fifty percent mark for years. Now that we've reached that benchmark, mobile sales are only going to go up. The challenge for sellers is how to optimize their listing to provide shoppers with the best possible mobile experience.

One way eBay is preparing for the uptick in mobile shopping is the elimination of all active content in listings by June of 2017. Included in the ban are Javascript, Flash plug-ins, and form actions. eBay says the use of these features can "negatively impact the user experience by inhibiting mobile purchasing, increasing page load times, and increasing security vulnerabilities."[1]

They also recommend sellers stop investing in custom store design "since this capability will [be] retired at a later date."

Eliminating custom store design is huge because it's what has distinguished eBay from Amazon. Many sellers have developed their businesses into multi-million dollar enterprises by branding their stores. After this capability goes away, growing your business is going to be much harder. It's going to make it harder for one seller to distinguish themselves from another, but it also gives us a significant clue as to what direction eBay is going.

Think commodity selling, the same as on Amazon, with one listing page and many sellers tagging along.

The switch to mobile and away from active content is good and bad. Good in that eBay is chasing market trends so that they can keep up with changing technologies; bad in that it marks the beginning of a new trend in eBay selling.

Make no mistake about there is going to be a shakeup for eBay sellers in the not-to-distant future. Examine your options now. Determine how it is going to impact your eBay business, and take appropriate actions.

---

[1] http://pages.ebay.com/sell/itemdescription/bestpractices.html

Getting back to mobile.

eBay created a mobile-friendly checker so that you can see how your items will display on portable devices. Check it out here. http://www.ebay.com/tools/sell/mobile-friendly-test

Tips to make your listings mobile-friendly

- eBay also suggests you should add the following HTML code to your listings. <meta name="viewport" content="width=device-width, initial-scale=1">. It tells the mobile browser how to "adjust the dimensions and scaling," so they display properly on mobile devices.
- If you run thousands of listings on eBay, you need to take action now and ensure your listing is compliant with the new mobile-friendly policies before eBay starts taking them down.
- If you have a custom listing template, consider eliminating it, or contact your listing designer so they can create one that complies with the new policies.
- Consider writing shorter item descriptions. eBay announced they would pull a 250 character description from your listing to display in mobile

searches. But, they did announce a way to display more text on mobile—write shorter listings, under 800 characters. If you do that, they will show your entire description.

Grow Your Sales With the Global Shipping Program

(Most of this section was first published in my book eBay Shipping Simplified: How to Store, Package, and Ship the Items You Sell on eBay, Amazon, and Etsy. For most eBayers, the transition to International shipping is scary at first—but it doesn't have to be. This section introduces you to the eBay Global Shipping Program—it's a pain-free way to get started selling internationally.)

Several years ago, eBay introduced its Global Shipping Program. It's an easy way for sellers to jump into international selling without having to worry about shipping rules, customs forms, etc.

If you've been itching to get started with international sales but were afraid of the extra work involved I suggest that you give it a shot using eBay's Global Shipping Program.

Many small sellers are terrified of international shipping. They've heard so many horror stories that they're scared to give it a shot. They don't want to fill out customs forms or worry about whether their package is going to make it to Timbuktu or not.

eBay has eliminated all of that grief for sellers who use their Global Shipping Program. Sellers list their items just like they usually would. When the item sells you ship it to an eBay shipping center in the United States.

Bing Badda Boom! As soon as it arrives at the shipping center, your responsibility for the shipment is over. From that point on, eBay and its shipping partners assume any liability for getting your package to its destination.

Here's how it works.

When you list your item for sale on eBay, check the box to include your item in the Global Shipping Program, and you're good to go.

Some categories don't qualify for inclusion in the Global Shipping Program. When you bump into these, eBay will flag the item and let you know. I do a lot of selling in the collectibles category. Collectibles manufactured before 1899 don't qualify, so I see this issue pop up quite often. The only way around it is to ship the item internationally yourself. I'll discuss this option in more detail later.

When an item sells using the Global Shipping Program, sellers can't send the buyer an invoice. eBay takes care of all this for you. The reason is you have no way of knowing what their shipping fee will be.

Once the customer pays, you will receive a payment notification along with the shipping address for your package. The easiest way to recognize a payment made through the Global Shipping Program is the address will include a long reference number.

Ship your item like you usually would. Include delivery confirmation, so you can ensure the shipping center received your item. Once you have confirmation the item was received, your part in the transaction is complete.

eBay's shipping partner—Pitney Bowes—will readdress your package, fill out all of the appropriate customs forms, and ensure delivery to the customer.

Overall the Global Shipping Program is an excellent way to increase your sales. During my peak selling period, international sales accounted for roughly thirty-five to forty percent of my eBay sales and profits.

If you're looking for an easy fix to grow your sales, opt into the Global Shipping Program and give it a shot.

Bonus Excerpt # 1 - Social Media Marketing Made Easy

(Here's an excerpt from one of my newest books, **eBay Business Expert**. This section focuses on how to use Social Media, especially Facebook, to grow your business. You can check the entire book out by following this link, eBay Business Expert.)

Social Media Marketing for eBay Sellers

Do you need to blow up social media to sell on eBay and Amazon?

Its sort of like asking, are you a glass is half full, or glass is half empty type of person. If you're a glass is half full type, you're going to scream "Damn right! You have to be on social media, because—that's where the people are." If you're a glass is half empty type, you're going to piss and moan "what's the point? I'm selling my stuff on eBay, not on Facebook and Twitter."

You probably see where I'm going with this.

Online sellers are divided on the need for social media, its uses, and its outcomes. Some vendors will tell you they couldn't have gotten where they are without it; others will say, "Why bother!" or "Hey! I tried it, and it didn't make any diff. My sales stayed the same."

I'm going to try not to take sides here. My goal is to give you the information you need to implement social media in your eBay business should you choose to do so.

My primary focus is going to be on Facebook, Twitter, and Pinterest because they are the three powerhouses behind social media today. Facebook and Twitter get a bigger mention because they are the social media sites everybody uses. Pinterest gets a larger mention because it is the one sellers say works best.

Does that mean you need to use all three? Or that you should focus exclusively on Pinterest because it's what works best for most sellers? No. You should start slow. Pick one or two social media platforms and spend ten or fifteen minutes on them two or three days a week.

A PEW University study on social media usage provides one more important piece of information for savvy online marketers—over half of the people who visit social media sites are active on more than one site. For marketers, the implication is clear. If you want to reach your primary customer base, you need to be active on several social media platforms. Using one social media platform isn't going to cut it. Think a minimum of two, maybe even three social media platforms, if you want to reach your target audience.

When you're first getting started, watch what other sellers in businesses like yours are doing on social media. Like some of their posts and start building your network. Make a few short posts. Put up a few pictures or some short videos. Rinse and repeat.

The key to success with social media is to post regularly, comment when someone likes or comments on one of your posts, and keep a conversation going with your followers. Over time you will develop a following of your own.

Don't try to move too quickly or fast-track your way to success. There are a lot of places on and off of eBay where you can purchase 500 or 1,000 likes. Don't be tempted. Phantom fans who don't comment on your posts, or like them, aren't going to do your business any good over the long haul.

Remember, it's not a contest to see who can get the most followers. It's all about getting the most followers who will engage with you regularly, and who will share your content with their friends and followers.

That's how you build your business using social media. Give more than you get, share content your followers like, enjoy, and can use. If you do this, sales will follow.

Social Media by the Numbers

A PEW University study published in 2014, reports Seventy-one percent of adults who use the Internet are on Facebook. Twitter, LinkedIn, Instagram, and Pinterest lag way behind with adult usage rates that fall somewhere between 23 to 28 percent.

Here are a few key takeaways for anyone planning to use social media to grow their online business.

- Thirty-one percent of seniors are on Facebook.
- Fifty-three percent of young adults age 18 to 29 are on Instagram. And, over half of these users visit the site daily.
- Women are three times more likely to use Pinterest than men. Forty-two percent of women who use the internet are on Pinterest, versus 13 percent of men.

If you need more help in choosing the right social media platform to reach your key demographics, check out the rest of the PEW University study.

Facebook users are aging, with a larger percentage of seniors over age sixty-five on the site. Women are more likely to frequent Facebook than men.

Twitter usage is higher among young adults ages eighteen to twenty-nine and falls off sharply among users at age forty-nine. Young adults and Afro-Americans are more likely to engage on Twitter.

Instagram has a high usage rate among young Americans ages eighteen to twenty-nine, and among Afro-Americans.

Pinterest users are primarily women, who tend to be college-educated and more affluent.

LinkedIn is used less than other social media sites but could be helpful if you are marketing to individuals between the ages of fifty to sixty-five. LinkedIn users also tend to be college graduates, with a higher annual household income.

The PEW University study does leave out one important group—teenagers.

If you're marketing primarily to teens, you need to check out a 2014 study by Piper Jaffray ... Taking Stock With Teens – Fall 2014.

Here is some of the information you will discover.

- Your message better look good on an iPhone, because 67 percent of teenagers either have or plan on getting an iPhone.
- Instagram and Twitter are the social media site most frequented by teens. If teens are your target

audience, you need to include more pictures, video, and music in your posts, and fewer words.

- Pinterest is the least used social media site among teens.
- Facebook is used by fifty percent of all teens but is not as popular as it was in the past.

One more important concept online sellers need to grasp is the people you want to reach, spend most of their day online. Many of them rarely, if ever leave social media sites, so if you don't engage with them there, you're not going to be able to sell to them—period.

Facebook

Facebook is the big kid on the block in social media marketing. It used to be the "in" site for kids, but now that it has gone mainstream, Facebook has become the primary social media platform used by marketers to reach women, age thirty-five to sixty.

If you haven't checked your Facebook News Feed lately, one of the first things you'll notice is the changes in the content you see. Many of the top posts shown in your News Feed are paid spots Facebook considers relevant to your interests. Your friend's posts are still there, intermixed with paid content Facebook finds relevant to you, and might make them a few bucks to boot.

Something else you need to understand is most Facebook users access the site only from mobile devices. You need to keep your posts short, with quick, easy to load pictures and videos. You should also check out every post you make to ensure it looks good on an Android or IOS (Apple) device.

Getting started

Facebook is all about engaging with other users. That means your primary goal is to provide content that makes users want to like, comment on, and share your posts.

How do you do that?

Look at the top posts in your News Feed; the one's users have liked and shared. The odds are they have at least one thing in common. Nine times out of ten, they are visually oriented, which means they contain pictures or videos.

Facebook pictures come in several varieties, but they all share one common trait. They're photos of a person, or a cute furry pet—maybe even a baby. They're of a person making a funny face, or stuck in a strange place, or doing something unusual. Other times it's a picture of someone famous along with one of their quotes.

If you pay attention, you will see dozens of similar pictures in your News Feed every week. Some of them are cartoon images with catchy phrases; others are quotes from famous people. Many are product images with tag lines that scream out – "new from" ... "on sale now" ... "check out our new line of."

Text-based images grab people's attention and garner a bunch of quick likes and shares. When you create these types of listings, you need to keep it legal. Don't just grab pictures you like off of the internet and add a snazzy quote. Make sure the image is copyright free. If you're in doubt, visit a clip art site and invest a few bucks in one-time rights to use the illustration. Two such clip-art sites I use all the time are Dollar Photo Club and Can Stock Photo. Most of the pictures on these websites cost under five bucks (less if you buy credits), and they're easy to manipulate using MS Paint so you can create unique images related to your topic.

Videos are hot on social media, and if your video catches on, it can go viral quickly and spread across the internet.

Make your videos tasteful and keep them focused on your product line. In my case, I sell old books and magazine articles. One video I include in all of my eBay listings is of Professor Puppet explaining my business and the types of items I sell. It helps people understand what my business is all about.

Other videos that would complement my product line would be reviews of historical books, how-to videos about book and magazine collecting, and special interest videos of time-sensitive events. Each of them would promote interest in the types of items I sell.

When I purchased my first Otterbox case, I couldn't figure out how to get it apart. Sure, it came with a short set of directions in a smattering of different languages, but that wasn't enough to help me install the case. To get my phone inside of my new Otterbox case, I had to search YouTube for a quick tutorial. (If you haven't discovered it, the trick to removing that thin outer shell is to slip a credit card underneath and pry it up. Thanks again, YouTube.)

A smart seller would have a similar video on his Facebook page, and in his eBay item listing. It's excellent customer service, and it's likely to be shared time and again, bringing customers back to your eBay listing and Facebook page. *Tip: if you decide to include someone else's video or photo in your listings or on your blog or website— get permission first. Contrary to popular belief, most pictures and videos on the internet are copyrighted, so it is illegal to reproduce them without proper authorization.*

If you sell men's, women's, or children's clothes every new season or product line you take on gives you the opportunity to add a new video to your Facebook page. If you're unsure how to do this, visit Lauren's Fab Finds for more ideas.

Create viral Facebook posts

There is a lot of advice available on how to create better Facebook posts. Here's a short list that should help you boost audience engagement.

- Keep your words to a minimum. Social media is constantly evolving, and the most commented on posts are visually oriented. If you want to maintain user engagement, keep any text short—80 to 120 characters should be the max.

- Don't link to stuff off Facebook. Facebook users prefer to stay in their own little world.
- Don't oversell. Facebook users are leery of marketing and are quick to steer away from sales pitches.
- Don't post the same content on Facebook that you do on other social media sites. Your followers expect new and exciting content, not yesterday's news, or recycled post from Twitter or your blog. Don't disappoint them.

How to Sell on Facebook

All of this begs the question, if Facebook users don't want to be sold to, how do you get them to buy your stuff?

That's a good question, and one smart sellers are working hard to crack. The key is to understand what brings people to social media sites in the first place.

According to an April 2013 report published in The Atlantic, the number one and three reasons people go on social media sites is voyeurism. Facebook is the perfect tool to spy on your neighbors and friends. The catch is: Facebook users are consensual Peeking Tom's. We give each other permission to poke their noses into our back doors.

The number two reason people say they visit social media sites is to relieve boredom. They've got nothing better to do, so they turn to Facebook, Twitter, and similar sites to live vicariously through others.

And, the final reason given for visiting social media sites is to message between friends.

So, there you have it.

- Voyeurism
- Boredom
- Messaging

If you are using social media to reach these people, you need to play to these needs.

Every post, picture, and video you place on social media sites should take people behind the scenes and give them a sneak peek of what your business or industry is all about. Make it personal, make it entertaining, show vulnerability, and poke fun at yourself.

At the same time, you need to make sure your posts are engaging. Encourage communication with your social media followers, and schedule time every day to follow up with them. If someone comments on one of your posts, respond to them, even if it's just to say "thanks" or "hi."

If you do these things, your posts will play into the reasons people visit social media sites.

Basics of Facebook Marketing

Create a Facebook Fan Page. Don't use your personal Facebook page. It's unprofessional, and it doesn't give you all the tools you need to engage with your followers.

Creating a Facebook Fan Page is easy. Go to https://www.facebook.com/pages/create.php.

That's going to bring up the following page where you select the category for your Facebook Fan Page.

The choices are:

- Local Business or Place
- Company, Organization or Institution
- Brand or Product
- Artist, Band, or Public Figure
- Entertainment
- Cause, or Community

Select the category that best describes your business. For most online sellers, it's going to be local business or place, or brand or product, depending on how you're trying to promote yourself. If you're an author, artist, or musician, choose an artist, band, or public figure. It's self-explanatory.

The next step is to set up your Facebook page and give it a name. Your page name should be a no-brainer. If you have a business name or eBay store name, that should be the name of your Facebook page. Make it easy for buyers to find you.

Make sure to fill out the about section, and provide a link to your eBay store so people can easily find you. Add appropriate keywords in the about section. In my case, I sell collectibles, so I would want to work in several of the following keywords, "vintage collectibles—magazine articles, prints, and advertisements." Sprinkling keywords into your page description makes it easier for search engines to locate your page.

Another neat feature you will find at the top of your page is the ability to *create a call to action button*. The button gives you a variety of choices, including—shop now, contact us, use the app, watch the video, book now, sign up, or play game. If you're an online seller, I'd suggest using shop now and linking to your eBay store and Sign up with a link to your email list sign up form. If you choose only one call to action, make it the sign-up form for your email list. It will give you the biggest bang for your buck over the long haul.

Create a fantastic Timeline Cover Photo (the rectangular image at the top of your Facebook page). It needs to reach out and grab viewer's attention. It could be one large photo or a collage of smaller photos showing yourself, your employees, or the products you sell. It may also be a good idea to add a tagline, or your business name, to your Timeline Cover Photo.

It's one of the first things people see when they come to your Facebook page, so you want to do your best to make it stand out and grab people's attention. With that said, here's my best advice—don't do it yourself. Hire a designer on Fiverr or Elance to put together a professional design for you.

You also need to create a profile photo. Some sellers use their logo; others use a picture of one of their better selling products. My suggestion is to use a selfie. Studies show people are more likely to engage with images of people, so give them what they want. Flash a big smile. If your audience would enjoy a joke—stick your tongue out at them or make a funny face. A lot of sellers get all fancied up and wear a suit or dress. That's okay, but my thought is you should present a more casual appearance. Dress like you usually would. It's easier for people to connect with you when you look like them.

Now it's time to start adding your first posts.

Deciding what to post scares a lot of people, but it's the easiest part of creating a Facebook page if you give it some thought. Think about yourself for a moment. What type of content do you enjoy engaging with on Facebook? Chances are you said—videos, pictures, and short entertaining posts.

That's the type of content you need to give your fan page visitors.

Create a couple of short two to three-minute videos that explain your business and talk about the products you sell, introduce your employees, interview a few of your customers, and let them say what they like about doing business with you. Post a few pictures of products you sell. Post a funny photo of your dog or cat playing with your computer or crawling out of a packing box. Post a picture of a hot new product you're getting ready to list.

If you're unsure what to post about, place yourself in your buyer's shoes and figure out what they'd like to know about your business or product line.

Sometimes your Facebook posts need a little more oomph to reach more viewers.

I know what you're thinking. "Hey! I'm on Facebook because it's free. What do you mean I have to spend money to get my posts seen?"

I know it's crazy, but it's true. Facebook has created a new way to make money, and part of it involves hiding your posts, or as they would have it—strategically placing them towards the top of a user's News Feed if you kick in a minor contribution to Zuckerberg and Company.

Here's what Facebook says about boosting your post. *"Boosted posts appear higher in your News Feed, so there's a better chance you will see them."*

You can promote any post—video, picture, or text. To get started, click on Boost post in the lower left-hand corner of the post. After you do that, select the audience demographics you want to see your post, your budget, and the length of time to boost the post.

Pretty simple so far, right?

In most cases, five to fifteen dollars should get you a big enough boost to reach your audience. If it's something special, like a new product launch, maybe budget forty or fifty dollars. As for the audience, try to narrow the focus to your prime demographic. If it's showing, your message is targeted to millions of readers try to narrow it down some. Shoot for something in the range of fifty to one hundred thousand for your target audience. For the time frame, you have a choice of one to seven days. If you boost it longer than two or three days you're going to find yourself pushing old news.

Create a Facebook Event to Promote Your Sale

A Facebook event may or may not work for you. The reason I say this is you can only create an event from your personal Facebook page, not from your Facebook fan page.

Don't get discouraged yet.

Promoting an event to your regular Facebook friends can help you introduce a new product line, or try out new ideas you usually wouldn't use with your regular customers.

Think of your event as a marketing test? It's a chance for you to try new things, and for your friends to get a hell of a deal. Promote it to them that way, and it will be a win-win situation for both of you.

If you're unfamiliar with Facebook events, the easiest way to think of it is as an online party invite. I've received them for family reunions, book launch events, and birthday parties. The great thing about creating a Facebook event is once you set it up, Facebook does all the work for you. It sends out the invites, collects RSVPs, and posts a reminder on the Facebook homepage for invitees.

The other cool thing is a Facebook event is super easy to create and manage.

Final takeaway

Facebook can be an excellent way to help grow your business. Like anything else, it can become a bottomless pit, sucking up all your time if you're not careful.

To be successful selling on Facebook, you need to:

- Have a plan. Know what you want to accomplish. Do you want to make more sales? Encourage email sign-ups? Engage more with customers?
- Budget 15 to 20 minutes a day three or four days a week and stick to that time limit.
- Be visual. Facebook users respond best to videos and pictures. Give them what they want.
- Don't over-post, or under-post. Three to five good posts a week is enough to get your message out there.
- Spend a few bucks to boost your posts, especially when you're first getting started. It will help you build your audience faster.

Bonus Excerpt # 2 – Bookkeeping Made Easy

(Here's an excerpt from one of my book, **eBay Bookkeeping Made Easy**. This section shows online sellers how to manage your sales, profits, expenses, and cash flow using GoDaddy Accounting. You can check the entire book out by following this link, eBay Bookkeeping Made Easy.)

GoDaddy Bookkeeping is available as an app you can download from eBay's applications bar. Amazon and Etsy sellers can check out the online version by visiting this link http://www.godaddy.com/accounting/accounting-software.aspx?isc=gooob012&ci=87249.

The service was formerly known as Outright and was taken over by GoDaddy. It's an online accounting solution that will serve the needs of most users. It automatically imports transaction data from your PayPal account and posts it to the proper categories. Users can also sync their business credit cards and checking accounts with the service.

For sellers conducting business on multiple platforms, GoDaddy Bookkeeping can import transaction data from eBay, Amazon, and Etsy. It also works with several invoicing services, including FreshBooks, Shoeboxed, and Harvest.

Here's the least you need to know. GoDaddy Bookkeeping is available on the *Applications* tab on your *My eBay* page. Hover your mouse over *Applications* until it shows Manage Applications, click on this and scroll through the list of applications until you come to *Outright*. Click on *Outright*, and select *Try It Free. (GoDaddy discontinued all free accounts as of December 21, 2014)*

GoDaddy Bookkeeping is available as a monthly ($9.99) or yearly ($99.00) subscription. Choose your poison, and follow the prompts to get started.

Overview

The first page you see is your account summary. It contains all the necessary information about your account. In the upper right corner, it shows your yearly profit or loss so you can tell at a glance where you stand. Below this is a graph that charts your income and expenses, a pie chart that shows your current month's expenses, and then a list of open invoices.

Below this is a section that shows Invoice Activity. Most online sellers aren't going to use this feature. eBay,

Amazon, Etsy, and your e-commerce storefronts invoice your clients for you. If you're running a side business where your customers pay through PayPal, GoDaddy can send invoices for you.

In the left-hand column, you'll see four small blue boxes. The first box is labeled *New This Week* and tracks your new sales and any uncategorized expenses. To view your new transactions or uncategorized expenses click on the number, and it will take you to your general ledger.

The *Money I Have Box* lets you check the balances in your accounts – PayPal, Amazon, and any bank accounts you have connected.

The Money I Owe box shows your liabilities or the money you owe. Some of the accounts shown here are your eBay balance, and money owed to Amazon and Etsy for seller fees.

The last box is labeled *Taxes*. It shows you several key tax indicators for your business. The first line shows your estimated quarterly tax payment, and when it is due. The mileage line shows your year to date mileage expenses. When you click on mileage, it takes you to your general ledger and lets you log your mileage. The last line shows your *Sales Tax Liability*, so you always know how much you owe.

Below the four blue boxes, you should see two blue bars. *Add Account* lets you add your various seller accounts,

PayPal Account, and any bank accounts you want to tie into GoDaddy Bookkeeping. *Refresh All* imports data from your connected accounts so that you're viewing the most recent information available.

If you scroll back up to the top of the page, you'll see your six control tabs – Overview, Income, Expenses, Reports, Taxes, and Manage. When you click on any of these they, open more program options.

Before I describe the control tabs, there's one other item I should cover. Sometimes a tan bar will appear just below the control tab. It shows program alerts or problems GoDaddy Bookkeeping may be experiencing with your account. When you click the Fix-It highlight, it will walk you through how to solve the problem so you can get your program up and running correctly again.

....

You can view your profit & loss statement anytime by clicking on the *view details* tab underneath where it says *(Year) Profit & Loss* on the GoDaddy Bookkeeping *Overview* page.

Your Profit & Loss statement gives you a quick overview of the financial health of your business. The top section shows your sources of income, and the bottom section details your expenses. The final line shows your "bottom line," or the actual profit or loss your business is making.

The default view for your P & L is the previous twelve months, but you have the option to change that any time you'd like. Scroll up to the top of the page under *Profit & Loss,* where you see *ending.* You can choose the ending month or year, or you can change the time-period today, week, month, quarter, or year. To return to the chart, select the chart icon on the right-hand side.

If you want to take a closer look at a transaction, all the items on your P & L are clickable. Select the one you want to examine, and it will take you to the general ledger page for that category.

Moving back down to the bottom of the page, you will see two tabs on the far-right side. Export lets you transfer P & L information to a Microsoft Excel file. Selecting print will give you a hard copy of your P & L.

Income

The income tab lets you manage your online income accounts. When you click on income, it takes you to your general ledger page for income, and you can view your most recent transactions.

Once again, all the transactions displayed are clickable. If you want to edit a transaction, select it, and make the needed corrections.

My suggestion is to set up categories so that you can track where your income sources. When GoDaddy Bookkeeping imports "income" transactions, it brings all of them under the general "sales" heading. If you're just selling on one venue, such as eBay or Amazon, that's not a problem. If you sell across multiple platforms, it's important to know where you're making sales. This way you can take corrective action if a sales venue is underperforming.

Every time you make a sale, GoDaddy Bookkeeping records it as two separate transactions. The merchandise portion records under the "Sales" heading. If you charged postage on the deal, it is filed under the heading "shipping income."

If you want to add additional sales categories, select a transaction, then scroll down the page until you see *Good to Know*. Off to the right-hand side, you will see a link labeled *Manage Categories*. It shows a chart of your current income categories. To add a category, select *New Income Category*. Categorize it as *Business* or *Nonbusiness*, and then name it. After this, select a tax category. To tie the category you created to sales; you would choose *gross receipts or sales*. Select *Create*, and it's ready to use.

To give you an idea of how to use this, I added the following categories to my income account – eBay sales, Amazon, Bonanza, *eBid*, bidStart, Kindle, Create Space, and Audible. By doing this, I can keep separate tabs on each of my sales channels. It gives me better control over my business and allows me to spot patterns early as they're beginning to emerge.

After you set up your income categories, you need to assign each transaction to the proper category. The easiest way to do this is from the Overview page. Select *view details* to see your P & L. Click on *sales* in the income section of your P & L. This will pull up all your unassigned items. Select each item separately and assign it to the proper account. This step is pretty straightforward and should take just a few moments every day.

Whenever you're working on your P & L, you should also examine your uncategorized expenses. They're listed at the bottom of the P & L, just before you see your bottom line. Most items are categorized when you import them, but there are usually a few uncategorized items, either because you purchased from a new supplier and GoDaddy Bookkeeping doesn't know how to classify it, or because the items may fit into several different expense categories. Click on the individual unclassified transactions and assign them to the proper category.

If you do this every time you open your program, it will only take a few minutes, and it will ensure your P & L is up-to-date and accurate.

Expenses

When you select expenses, it brings up the general ledger view for your business expenses.

You can set up personalized categories to customize GoDaddy Bookkeeping to fit your needs. Select an individual expense to enter the edit mode. Scroll down the page until you see the heading *Good to Know*. Move your mouse to the far right of the page and click on *manage categories*. Select *new expense category* and follow the prompts. Categorize the expense as a business or nonbusiness expense and name it. Scroll through the *tax category list* to tie your new expense to the proper category, and then select *Create*.

I would suggest setting up custom categories for your internet and cell phone providers, storage space rental, etc.

I find it useful to lump a few expense categories together. The main category I do this with is postage. I throw all my shipping costs there – boxes, packing tape, stay free mailers, peanuts, you name it. The reason I do this is it makes it easier to compare my shipping expenses and shipping income. If my shipping income is equal to, or more, than my shipping costs, I know I'm on the right track. When they get out of whack, it's time for an intervention to determine what went wrong.

With my other expenses, I monitor them to ensure they're consistent from month-to-month. If one month is way up without a similar bump in sales, it's time to investigate what happened. Maybe it's a one-time buy I had the opportunity to make; sometimes, a number was entered wrong. The critical thing is to watch your numbers and react ASAP when you see that something is out of whack.

Reports

When you select reports, it brings you to your Profit and loss statement. GoDaddy Bookkeeping always shows you the chart first. Select *view as a table* to see your P & L Statement.

If you're running a business, you should know these numbers forward and backward. Growth is good, but I like to see consistent numbers across the board.

When I'm comparing my book sales numbers, the first thing I do is compare them with the last few months. If sales seem unusually low, I examine last year's numbers to see if it's a seasonal trend. You should do the same thing.

Online sales are always slower in summer. They typically pick up by late August and run strong through spring. February and October can be iffy – they can go either way.

The first half of November can be the same way, waiting for Christmas buying to kick in.

Key point: Use your P & L to help forecast fluctuations in your business. Study it for trends, where sales are increasing or decreasing, or where expenses are rising. Put on your detective hat and figure out what's happening. Doing this will make you a better business person and help your business to grow stronger over the long haul.

Taxes

The taxes section helps you with three specific areas.

- It provides your Schedule C information to make tax time a breeze. Just transfer over the numbers, and you're ready to file. Keep in mind; you're still going to need a tax advisor, or a good tax program, like TurboTax Business, or HR Block Business. GoDaddy Bookkeeping doesn't figure the home office deduction, tax credits, etc. They provide you with the raw numbers to fill out your Schedule C.
- GoDaddy tracks your sales taxes due, so it's easy to file and submit your state reports. If you have eBay, Amazon, and Etsy set up to collect sales tax in your state, GoDaddy Bookkeeping will track all the information for you.

- Every time you log into your account, you can see your estimated tax payments and the date they are due. This way, the due date and the amount you owe won't sneak up on you.

Manage

When you select manage, it displays a list of all the accounts you have connected to GoDaddy Bookkeeping. If any of the accounts have errors, you will see a tan bar. Click on the blue *Fix It* links to take care of account issues.

If you want to connect more accounts, select *Add an Account* at the top of the page

Good to know

You can reassign categories if something is categorized incorrectly.

Most often, when this happens, it's because the program does not recognize how to classify the transaction. To fix the problem select the item that needs to be categorized. At the far right, it will show the uncategorized item. Select the correct category from the drop-down box, and press save.

You will also need to re-categorize items when you make a non-business related purchase. GoDaddy Bookkeeping has a *personal expense* category you can assign the item to, so it is removed from your business records. If you sell an individual item and receive payment for it through your PayPal account, you can reassign it to the *personal income* category.

Best advice

Keep a close eye on your accounting program. Update it every few days. It's easier to catch errors when just a few items are displayed. If you let it go too long, an extensive list of articles to re-categorize can seem overwhelming.

Bonus Excerpt # 3 – eBay Subject Matter Expert

(This is an excerpt from my book eBay Subject Matter Expert: 5 Weeks to Becoming an eBay Subject Matter Expert. It will give you a different perspective on selling and attracting new customers.)

What I am going to outline here is a five-step program that will put you on the road to becoming an eBay Top Rated Seller, but it will also make you an expert in your chosen field of sales.

The great thing is this plan will work for you whether you are new to eBay or an established seller. Keep in mind; trust is earned, not given. The easiest way to earn trust is to help people without being concerned about payback.

eBay provides two tools to help sellers build trust and authority: Guides and reviews.

A **guide** is a tutorial on how to do something. It can be as simple as one sentence. "This was the greatest product ever; I lost ten pounds in under a week using it." Or it can go on for thousands of words and tell people everything they need to know about replacing the battery in a Kindle Fire HD, or it could be the recipe for a new chocolate-covered flavored bacon cookie you developed. The possibilities are endless, as eBay will let you write a guide on just about any topic under the sun.

A **review** is your opinion of a book, movie, or product you have used. Once again, the sky is the limit. eBay will let you write a review of anything you want.

The great thing is every time someone reads your guide, eBay gives them a minimum of two ways to find your products. At the top of each guide, eBay displays a header with your user id, the number of feedbacks you have, and a link to your store. Under that, they show three products related to the guide. If you're lucky, sometimes they will feature one or more of your products there; it just depends on how close of a match they are.

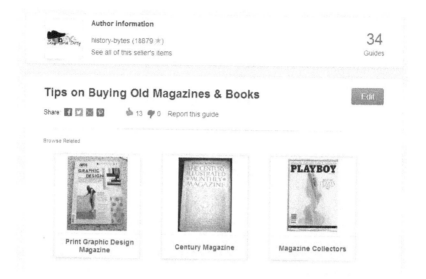

Tips on Buying Old Magazines & Books   Edit

Share: 🄵 🄳 ✉ 🄿   👍 13   👎 0   Report this guide

Browse Related

Print Graphic Design Magazine

Century Magazine

Magazine Collectors

Many times, eBay will display three items for sale from the author's store below the guide. Buyers can scroll through a list generated by eBay, or they can click into any of your items that tickle their fancy.

Either way, it's a win for you because it offers several more ways for buyers to find your listings. The cool thing is when they discover you this way, they already know you from your guide and understand you are an expert in what you are selling. As a result, they're more likely to do business with you.

It's like the story of the car salesman who rushes out to greet you as soon as you hit the new car lot. The minute he asks, "How can I help you?" or "What are you, folks, looking for today?" – Your defense shields immediately go up, and you blurt out "just looking," and start to move away. It's a natural reaction. Everybody does it.

If that same salesman starts by saying, "That's a nice looking Camaro, you're driving. I bet you had some great times in it." You're likely to share a story about the time you were speeding down that old country road, and—

You get the idea. Your guide warms your customers up and lets them know you're a real person who's concerned about them and willing to help.

It's your opening line, or you're ice breaker. It gets your customer's attention.

Google indexes eBay guides and reviews, so anyone searching for the topic has an excellent chance to find you when they do an internet search.

Author's Items for Sale

See all of this seller's items

1869 South American Earthquakes Arica Peru Equador
$25.99
Buy It Now

1888 Roosevelt Remington Ranch Life in Far West
$19.99
Buy It Now

1895 Frances Willard Women's Christian Temeprance Union
$19.99
Buy It Now

How to write a guide

Writing a guide can seem like a formidable task, especially if it is the first one you've ever attempted, but it doesn't have to be that hard.

The easiest way to get started is to approach it like you're talking to a friend. Tell them what you want to say. Include all the necessary details, and share a few stories about what happened when you or someone you know used this approach.

That's all there is to it.

If you're considering a more extensive guide, write a short outline first. It will help you organize what you want to say and make sure you've included all the necessary details.

If I was going to write a guide about how to ship your item internationally, my outline might look something like this:

- Introduction
- Why listen to me/my qualifications
- How to tweak auction to add international selling
- How to pick a shipping method/carrier
- Where to get help
- What to tell buyers/set delivery expectations
- Legal disclaimers

- Final words of encouragement

My outline is short, to the point, and will help keep me on track when writing my guide. Your outline should be flexible enough to let you add or subtract ideas once you get started working on it.

The main thing to remember when writing is not to stress out over grammar, spelling, sentence structure, etc., etc.

Instead, focus on offering high quality, actionable information readers can use to enhance their knowledge or perform a new task, such as learning how corner damage affects the grading of 1950's baseball cards. Readers will overlook a lot if you can give them useful, actionable information.

What's that you say? You're not sure what to write about.

You need to get in the habit of writing. People are desperate for knowledge on just about any topic. If you write it, someone is going to find it and read it.

Let's go back to the example of someone selling baseball cards. Possible topics are new releases, card grading services, star players, trades, football – baseball – basketball in season. "How about those Bears?" You can talk about your favorite team or maybe a favorite series of cards. Did you see a major league game as a kid that got you started collecting? Talk it up. Perhaps you went to school with a kid who's a star player for the Cubs or White Sox. Tell people what he was like back then.

What do you collect? Who is your favorite player? Maybe you could pick two or three players a week and write guides detailing their careers or some of the cards that have featured them.

The possible topics are endless.

Just as important as the things you should write about are the things you shouldn't. A lot of sellers write guides about new products they've listed. It doesn't make much sense. They tell you, "Hey, we just got in a 'lot' of new Pokémon Games," or "I just listed a retro yellow polka dot bikini."

These aren't proper guide topics.

A better way to approach it would be to write a review of Pokémon White or Pokémon Silver. Or put together a guide discussing the various Pokémon games, when they were released, and the differences in them. This information would help to set you apart as a gaming expert, especially if games are one of the main products you carry.

Hopefully, that helps you understand the difference. A review gives your opinion about, or your experience using a particular product; a guide shares information about a particular subject. A guide helps people to learn more about something.

If you say, "Hey! I just got in a bunch of so and so," it makes you look like a spammer. It doesn't add to the conversation or help anyone.

Writing guides isn't hard.

It's just a matter of getting started. The more content you create, the more people are going to read your guides and discover your items on eBay.

I know, sometimes it seems like you're taking a stab in the dark. But I guarantee you if you keep posting guides, people are going to find your listings. They're going to buy from you and tell their friends about you.

It's happened to me hundreds of times. It can, and will, happen to you.

Product Reviews

If you want to sell, more products take the time to write thoughtful reviews about your experiences with different books, movies, and products.

Everyone, no matter whether they are spending one dollar or a thousand dollars hesitates about whether to click the buy button or not. It's human nature.

A useful review eliminates some of this tension and can make customers more willing to give that new product a try. Look at Amazon. They built an entire business from letting everyday people post reviews of books, products, and movies. They know people need reassurance that they are making the right decision. They prefer that reassurance comes from other people just like themselves, not from some guy who makes his living writing reviews.

That's why the eBay platform for writing reviews is so essential for growing your business, but only if you approach it the right way.

Reviews should be more folksy and personal than a guide. You want to inject a lot of your personality into them, especially when you are reviewing movies and books. Connect with your customers; share information about yourself. If they like what you say and they enjoy your selection, they will be back for more of your words of wisdom.

The critical takeaway is to inject as much of your personality as you can into each review. Make it fun to read. Be honest. If you didn't like the movie or book tell people, but explain why you didn't like it. For example: "Overall it was a great show, but I didn't like the way it ended. There was no closure." "I was lost through the whole thing. I couldn't figure out why..."

If you're reviewing more serious works, like books on history or science, you should keep a more professional tone. Talk about the premise of the book, how the author presented his topic, and if you feel qualified – tell readers what you think. Does the book make sense; does the conclusion match the evidence the author presented; if not, what do you think he (or she) should have done differently.

Don't be afraid to tell people where the author went wrong. Academics do this all of the time. They use reviews to add another piece to the puzzle and get in their two cents worth. If you plan to write a lot of scientific or academic book reviews, I would recommend **They Say / I Say** by Gerald Staff and Cathy Birkenstein.

The same thing goes if you're reviewing products.

Take a few minutes to introduce people to it and what it does. If there's a lot of hype surrounding the product, tell people why you bought it, and what your expectations were. Next, explain what happened. Did you have a good, bad, or mixed experience? Share your feelings about the product, and make a recommendation.

Should readers buy it or take a pass on it.

Remember, the whole idea is to encourage people to purchase the product from you, so you want to keep your reviews on a more positive note. If I'm on the borderline, I say. "That's my opinion. Read it yourself and let me know what you think."

If you think about it, every eBay store is going to have the new movie release from Tom Hanks or Sandra Bullock, and you can only go so low on the price. If you write a review to let people know what you thought about the movie, including the good, the bad, and the ugly – They just might click on your store to see if you have it for sale.

If buyers like what you say, they will check back to get your take on that new movie or book.

Don't let them down.

Bonus Excerpt # 4 -Use Kickstarter to Grow Your Business

Most eBay businesses get started with little or no money out of pocket. Sellers begin by listing items they already have around the house. As time goes by, they decide eBay is a pretty decent way to make a few extra bucks.

The next step may be to sell a few things for friends and neighbors. More often than not, they check out a yard sale, garage sale, or local estate sale and then see what's available at local thrift stores.

If these sellers need financing, it most often comes from their credit cards.

Up until now, that's been the extent of business credit available to eBay sellers. Banks aren't too helpful when they hear the words "eBay" and "business" used together. All too often, negative connotations come to mind, and the banker ends up telling you it's "a great concept, but ____." (You can fill in the blank.)

Kabbage is another financing option available to eBay and Amazon sellers. Kabbage offers small business loans from $500 to $100,000 to online sellers based upon sales data from their eBay and Amazon accounts. Their finance rates aren't cheap. I think I paid $90.00 in interest and fees on a $500 loan. The good thing is you get the money quickly—most often within an hour or less of applying. It's deposited directly into your PayPal account, and payments deducted from your PayPal account.

If you have a brick and mortar location or connection with a local banker, more options may open up to you, but for most sellers—the only choice is to use their credit cards or to get a short-term loan from Kabbage.

. . . .

Crowdfunding is one of the newer financing options available.

At its most basic level, crowdfunding is asking a group of like-minded persons to back you. In essence, you tell them, I have this cool idea for a new way to sell Manga on eBay, but I need a little cash to get it started. In return for their support (money), you reward backers with different incentives. For $5.00 you may give them a shout out on your home page or a free digital download. For $25.00 you could offer the first edition of a new Manga, for $250, you could give a hand-signed poster from a semi-famous artist, or for $2500, the reward could be an invitation to the online opening of your new store. Or maybe you could offer to feature the backer's face somewhere in your store graphics.

The most successful crowdfunding campaign to date was the Veronica Mars Kickstarter in 2013. Producers raised nearly six million dollars from 91,000 backers who couldn't get enough of the TV series. $25 sponsors received a digital download of the movie; $200 backers received a poster hand-signed by the cast, and one lucky $10,000 backer received a speaking role in the film.

In effect, crowdfunding is the coming together of people and an idea. It's a collaboration to make something happen.

For eBay sellers, it's a tougher sell because you're raising money for a commercial product with just one purpose in mind—to make more money. So if you intend to attract backers, you need to craft one hell of a story.

The Least You Need to Know

The first thing you need to know about Kickstarter https://www.kickstarter.com/ is you're either "all in, " or you're "all out."

If you set your goal at $10,000, you don't get one cent if you don't raise at least $10,000. If you raise $9,999, you're out of luck. None of those credit cards get charged, and you walk away empty-handed.

Think it can't happen to you?

More than 55 percent of the projects listed on Kickstarter don't reach their goal. The numbers are even gloomier when you look at all crowdfunding platforms—25 percent of all projects listed don't receive even one cent in backing.

How scary is that?

I'm not telling you this to discourage you from running a Kickstarter; instead, I'm trying to help you understand how important it is to have a plan and thoroughly research your project before you get started.

The first thing you need to know about Kickstarter is it's not about getting money to fund your business. It's about getting money to finance a project.

So if you need to raise $100,000 so you can start selling iPhones on eBay, it's not going to happen. Not on Kickstarter anyway. If your business makes custom cases for the iPhone 5 and 6 with custom graphics or a hot new design you created, Kickstarter might be the ticket to help you launch your business.

The reason custom iPhone cases could get funded is it's a unique project. If your graphics are cool enough, or if the design is unique and stands out head and shoulders over what's available on the market—it just may go viral and grab the interest of backers.

Here's another example.

If you ask for $25,000 to start an online CD store, you're unlikely to attract any backers, except your mom and your Uncle Bob (and even they may be a hard sell). But, if you're the lead singer in a local or regional band and you run a Kickstarter to raise the cash to press your first CD to sell in your eBay store that could grab a whole lot of backers, as would a CD of local school kids singing local folk songs or Christmas carols.

Do you see the difference?

A Kickstarter is something you use to launch a one-time project, not to fund an ongoing business. That's not to say you can't create a string of similar projects that turn into an entire product line for your eBay store. If you run a successful Kickstarter to fund a CD for a local band, there's nothing to stop you from running another Kickstarter for the same band's next album, or an entire series of albums for many local or regional musicians.

It's all about breaking your goal down into a series of attainable projects.

Getting funded

What if you run a Kickstarter and nobody backs you? It'd be embarrassing, wouldn't it? Remember back to those statistics I gave you earlier—25 percent of all crowdfunding projects never receive one penny in backing, and 55 percent of Kickstarter's never launch.

Here's a tip I heard over-and-over again from successful and unsuccessful Kickstarter's. Ask for the smallest amount of money necessary to get your project off the ground. We all want a million dollars, but if ten thousand dollars will help your project achieve liftoff, set your goal at ten thousand dollars. You may get a whole lot more, you may not, but if you hit $10,000 Kickstarter is going to run all those credit cards, and ka-ching! You're in the money!

That's the great thing about Kickstarter. They don't shut the faucet off when you reach your goal. Some projects go on to raise five or ten times their initial objective. And, that's another thing successful Kickstarter's say, try to have enough momentum going into your project so that you can meet your goal in the first three days. That way, anything else you take in is just frosting on the cake.

What You Need to Know

- Kickstarter reviews and vets all projects. Your odds of being approved are roughly 50 percent. If you've got a sustainable idea, but they think it needs a little work, the folks at Kickstarter will give you tips to make it more fundable.
- You need to choose a time frame for your Kickstarter. It can be as short as one day or as long as sixty days. Keep in mind—longer is not always better. Kickstarter says projects attract the most backers during their first three days and last three days, so it's those six days that make or break your project. Most sellers I've talked with say thirty-days is the sweet spot, any longer and you encourage backers to procrastinate and possibly miss funding your project.
- Remember, you're asking people to help you, but it's not going to work if you come right out and beg for help. Instead, you need to show backers how your project can help other people, or help them. Make sure your supporters understand it's not just about the money; it's about being part of something new and exciting—like bringing back Veronica Mars.

- Video is the key. A creative video is impressive, but it's more important to get out there in front of the camera and be yourself, be genuine, and explain your project in terms people can relate to, and understand

- One video isn't going to be enough. You need a series of videos. Create one or two videos that explain your project. Try to get a couple of your backers to talk about your project, and what excited or intrigued them about it. As your project progresses, create several videos to update people on your status—" we're almost there." "We're so close, and every donation you make will bring us that much closer to hitting our goal." Or, "We just created a new stretch goal so be sure to check out our new reward levels." Or, "here's what hitting our new level will let us achieve."

- Be sure to tell backers why it's important for them to help you. Let them know why you need their help, what's in it for them, and what will happen when you hit your goal. Remember, if backers don't understand why they need to contribute, your project isn't going to get off the ground.

- Creative rewards are essential to get more supporters and getting your project funded. You need several different levels of rewards to achieve liftoff. At the low end, you can give a shout out on your blog or website, or offer a digital download. The midrange--$25 to $50—is the perfect spot to provide a custom t-shirt, an autographed book, or something with a higher perceived value. At the high end, over $100—you need unique rewards that make backers feel they're a part of something special, and their contribution is going to make it happen. The best way I heard it described was to decide what it's going to take to get someone to give up a latte, or dinner and a movie out, and help them justify why they should forgo some of life's little pleasures to back you instead.

- Professional quality pictures are essential. You've got to show your project in its best light—up-close, with people using it if possible. Make sure your photos and videos tell the story. Most backers are just going to look at your photographs and decide based on what they see. Others will decide by looking at the photos and videos whether they're going to read your text to get the rest of the story.

- If things go wrong and you don't hit your goal, it's not the end of the world. Be a gracious loser. Email your backers and thank them for their support. If you lined up a different source of funding in the meantime, let supporters know your project is going to move forward despite the setback on Kickstarter. Whatever you do, let your backers know what's next—a new Kickstarter, or maybe a scaled-back version of your project.

- Whether your project gets funded or not, take time out to analyze your Kickstarter. What went well?

Where did it all fall apart? It's not a total loss if you can learn from your mistakes. If no one backed your project, you might need to approach it from a new angle, or you may decide it's time to move on and try something different. It may be that even though you didn't hit your goal, you created enough publicity that you can pick up commercial financing or a new set of backers. Whatever you do, don't just throw in the towel without taking the time to analyze what happened.

Kickstarter – The Nuts & Bolts

Setting up a Kickstarter is pretty straightforward. Navigate your way to https://www.kickstarter.com/. Click on *learn more*, and then *start a project*. Kickstarter will show you the following sentence—"I want to start a_____ project called _____." Fill in the two blanks, and you're ready to start.

There are fifteen categories to choose from for your project type: arts, comics, crafts, dance, design, fashion, film and video, food, games, journalism, music, photography, publishing, technology, and theater.

The most successful categories are film and video, music, design, games, art, and publishing. What that means is if you choose a project that fits into one of these categories, you are more likely to get funded.

Next, you need to give your project a title. Don't try to be cutesy or clever. Instead, say what your project is all about. If you're a local band, title it "Davenport, Iowa River Rats premiere CD," or "Pictorial History of Black Hawk State Park."

After you enter the title, it takes you to the product page. This is where the magic starts. So, before you begin, make sure you understand what each step is asking you to do.

The first thing you need to do is upload a project image. This is the money shot. It's how people will judge your project. When potential backers see it, it needs to grab their attention and entice them to keep scrolling down the page. Kickstarter recommends your picture should be at least 1024x768 pixels and have a 4:3 aspect ratio.

Next, you get a chance to revise your title. You've got sixty characters to work with, so make them count. Don't mince words or try and be clever. Your title needs to be clear, concise, and contain two or three keywords that tell people what your project is all about. Hint: Your title is searchable by keyword along with your name, so this is one of the ways people are going to find you. Make it easy for backers to find your Kickstarter, and you will attract more donations.

The next space asks for a short blurb—just 135 characters. It needs to whet someone's appetite and make them want to keep scrolling down the page to discover what's next?

After this, pick a category and sub-category for your project. And, then you set your location. I think the location feature is one of Kickstarter's real strength. Backers can search projects to locate Kickstarter's in their hometown, state, or region, so you want to make sure they can key in on you.

After location, you need to pick a funding duration. That's just a fancy way of asking how long you want your Kickstarter to run. Thirty days is the suggested sweet spot, but you can make it as short as one day or as many as 60 days. Just keep in mind what we talked about earlier—most backers pick up on a project in its first three days and its final three days. These are the days you need to be pushing the hardest.

The final thing you need to do in this section is set your funding goal. Remember, you may want $100,000, but if $10,000 will launch your project, that's the amount you should set for your goal. Kickstarter is an "all or nothing" environment. If you don't reach your funding goal, you don't get anything—no matter how much was pledged.

That's as far as I'm going to take you with setting up your Kickstarter. They provide an excellent section to walk you through telling your story. You can access it by following this link
https://www.kickstarter.com/help/handbook/your_story.

Getting the Word Out

So, you've created a Kickstarter now what?

Just about every person I talked with who created a Kickstarter offered the same advice. Running your campaign is a full-time job. It requires planning, research, and constantly getting out there 24 / 7 to share your story.

Here's one thing most people don't understand. Kickstarter is only going to bring you ten to fifteen percent of your backers. It's up to you find the other 85 percent of your funding. Sounds sort of like what I told you about eBay, doesn't it? Kickstarter is a platform to conduct your crowdfunding campaign.

Getting the word out is up to you.

Here the top ten tips I uncovered to help you run a more successful Kickstarter.

- Build your tribe before you get started. To be successful, you need an email list and a substantial Twitter and Facebook following. That way when you start your Kickstarter, you can have them jump in and be your initial wave of backers.
- You need to research other Kickstarter's in your category to see how they're approaching things. Learn from what they're doing right; eliminate the mistakes they're making.
- Go local. If you're a local band, musician, writer, manufacturer whatever, reach out to the local media. Get as much publicity as you can. Submit press releases. Get on local TV and radio programs, and seek out opportunities for write-ups in the newspapers and regional magazines.

- Reach out to niche bloggers. Offer to do interviews, guest posts, or provide free content for them. If possible, work out a trade where you can do something for them if they email their list with details about your Kickstarter.
- Ask family, friends, and work associates to help get the word out on their social networks. You never know, they may have the ear of an influencer who can help your Kickstarter go viral.
- Rewards are essential to your success. Kickstarter says $25.00 is the most common backing, while $70.00 is the average pledge. What that tells you is you need to focus a lot of sweet rewards in the $25.00 to $75.00 range. You don't have to break the bank, but give them a high perceived value—a special edition of a CD, book, or print, a hand-signed t-shirt, or whatever you feel your audience will appreciate more than the backing you are requesting.
- Keep adding content to your Kickstarter page. Research shows many backers sneak two or three peeks at your story before they decide to back you. Be sure to add new content, especially more videos and pictures. Update your page to let backers know how close you are to reaching your goal or about new stretch goals and rewards if you've already achieved your initial objective. The main thing is to keep backers in the loop.

- Back a few projects before you post yours. It provides social proof that you play well with others, and Kickstarter has a spot at the top of each project page that shows how many projects you've backed. If that spot is blank, it makes you appear somewhat like Mr. Scrooge. People will think you're looking for handouts, but you're not willing to help out. "Bah! Hum-bug, Mr. Scrooge!"

- You need to show why you're the best person to complete the project you posted. Tell backers what's unique about you. What makes you the right guy to get this thing done? Have you tackled a similar project? Share your motivation, so people will know you're the right guy or gal for the job.

- You can lose, and still, come out a winner. Just because you didn't get the funding, you asked for doesn't make you a loser (it just means you'll have to try a little harder). A successful Kickstarter can generate a lot of publicity that will help grow your business down the line. It can be a great conversation starter. "We didn't get funded, but we got a lot of great responses." Or, "we learned..." It might provide the feedback you need to come back with an improved and even better product. I also talked with a gentleman who wasn't asking for money. Alan Fine's niche is ghost stories, and he created a website that asked backers to contribute ghost stories rather than cash. If you want to explore this option in more detail, here is Alan Fine's webpage http://www.catalystghoststories.com/#!no-cost-crowdfunding/c43i.

Bonus Excerpt # 5 – Do These Things First

From my experience, there are certain things sellers can do that will make more successful.

If you're a seller teetering on the brink of success instituting some of these changes could give you the extra nudge you've been looking for to break into the big time. If you're a new seller, there's no better time to get started doing things the right way. You don't have any bad habits to break. Just jump in and get started.

Keep in mind—this is stuff that has worked for me with the items I sell. Not everything will work for you. Keep doing what works for you—adjust or discard the rest.

1. Remove all HTML code from your listings.

eBay's Cassini Search does not play well with HTML code—especially when you have HTML code in the listing header.

I love a fancy listing template that has a great design and perfectly formatted pictures, but what I like even better is listening to the cash register ding on my eBay app.

If your sales are down, and nothing you do is working—strip the header out of a few listings, remove all of that fancy formatting and templates out of a few more. Then see what happens.

If unformatted listings allow you to make more sales, that's the way to go. By doing this, you can decide for yourself what works and what doesn't.

2. After you post a listing, view it on your smartphone and tablet. If you have trouble viewing your listing re-work it, or cancel the listing and start over.

The internet today is all about mobile. People always check their phones, tablets, and Kindles all day long for new emails, tweets, and Facebook updates. Last Christmas, nearly thirty percent of holiday shopping took place on mobile devices. This year that number is expected to be closer to fifty percent.

If you don't optimize your listing for mobile, you're going to miss out on fifty percent of the customers searching for your items.

At the end of the day, when you finish listing items, check some of them on your smartphone or iPad. Ensure that your items appear in search and are optimized for mobile viewing. If you inserted your photos into your listing using HTML code or a listing application like Auctiva or Ink

Frog your pictures are going to appear small, and they will be hard to view. If you posted them using eBay's list, your item page, your photos would expand to fill the entire device screen, and potential buyers will be able to use the arrow keys to move between one image and another.

Ask yourself which format you're more likely to buy from, and make the appropriate changes.

3. Get straight to the point. Less is better. People are in a hurry to get things done. The easier you make it buy from you, the more stuff you're going to sell.

People are lazy. They read auction descriptions the same way they read blog posts and everything else on the internet. They scan the description for words that catch their fancy. They cruise through bullet points for a quick overview. They glance at the captions for pictures.

If they run into a big blob of text, they're going to click the back arrow button and move on to the next listing. White space, bullet points, and bold headings are your allies in making more sales.

4. Include more and better pictures.

A good fifty percent of buyers make their decision just by looking at the pictures in your listing. They don't have time to read, or they don't want to read your item description. Many foreign buyers can't read or understand your description. They rely solely on the pictures you include to make their decision.

Some sellers play to this. They include lots of close up pictures and encourage buyers to check the images and decide for themselves if the item meets their needs.

5. Focus on the 80 /20 rule. Concentrate on selling the 20% of articles that bring you the most profit. Scrap the slow sellers.

If you're like most sellers, a few of your items account for the majority of your sales volume.

If you've got an eBay store, the odds are you have hundreds, maybe thousands of items languishing in there. Maybe ten or twenty sell every month, but the rest of them sit there—festering. They suck up your monthly free listings and cost you additional listing fees. They taunt you into working extra hours, hoping they'll be that one other sale you need to buy a new iPhone or an extra appetizer at lunch.

Quit playing the longshots. Aim and start focusing on sure things. Concentrate on the twenty percent of items that sell the best, don't waste time and money on listings that rarely sell.

6. Don't try to reinvent the wheel. It's great to find a new product that no one else has and will sell like hotcakes. There are very few items like that. If you

focus all your time on looking for the newest greatest thing, you're going to miss out on a lot of sure things.

Everyone wishes they could go back in time and be the first guy in on the Hula Hoop craze, the Pet Rock, or the Chia Pet, but—those kinds of things are a one in a million shot. If you concentrate all of your effort on the long ball, you're going to miss the sure hits along the way.

Sure, catching the wave on a new fad can make you wealthy and famous, but selling sure things like denim jackets, vintage toys, etc. will keep the cash registers ringing day in and day out. They'll put food on the table and gas in your tank.

Chasing fads will suck up listing fees, the time you could spend posting profitable items, and free time you could have invested with your family and friends.

7. Don't beat a dead horse. Things run out of gas. They stop selling for one reason or another. Know when to call it quits and move on to a new niche.

Good things come to an end.

I've spent the last fifteen years selling vintage magazine articles, prints, and advertisements. They've been slugging along in low gear since the recession of 2008. eBay's move to fixed-price listings is another nail in their coffin. Sales are down, selling prices are down, and profits are down.

I'm beating a dead horse.

I've got two choices—reinvent myself, or reimagine my product line. It's hard. We've been together for fifteen years. There's still money coming in—sometimes thousands of dollars a month, but it's nothing like it was.

The challenge for 2015 is to reinvent my business and carve out a new niche.

What about you? If you're beating a dead horse, do you have the plan to put it down, or breathe new life into it?

8. Spend more time on customer follow up. Chit chat. Shoot the shit. It's going to help you build a relationship with customers, and sell more stuff.

Getting to know your customers doesn't take that long. You need to make it a regular part of your business day. When someone inquires about an item you have for sale—answer their question. Take a few minutes to thank them for contacting you. Talk up your item and your product line. Ask how they're going to use it, and what other things they'd like to see you offer.

If it's close to a holiday—wish them a "Merry Christmas!" or a "Happy Easter!" If you want to be politically correct, wish them a "happy holiday season." Getting to know your customers only takes a few moments, but it gives buyers a warm and fuzzy feeling about doing business with you.

9. Try new things. Complacency has killed more companies than anything else. Try selling at least

one new product every week. At the end of the year, if only five of them work, you've still got a stronger product line.

Products and entire product lines go stale. Things become obsolete. People become outdated if they don't change. Think back to the guys you knew in high school and college. How many of them are still reliving their glory days? It's great to spend five or ten minutes with them and reminisce, but then you start to get this queasy feeling— this guy's not going anywhere. He's stuck in the past.

Products are the same as people. They get stuck in a certain period.

If you're not selling nostalgia, you need to cut the strings and try new things. It will make your product line stronger and force you to become a better seller.

10. When a buyer protection case gets filed against you, put aside any personal feelings, or any thoughts the customer is trying to put one over on you. Pull the trigger, and give them a full refund—especially with low dollar amount items. You'll feel better, and it'll make you look better with your customers and with eBay.

Think of it this way. In the larger scheme of things— what's twenty, fifty, even a hundred dollars compared to everything you sell on eBay? You may be in the right. The customer may be taking advantage of you, but—is it worth lowering your ranking in search or having your selling privileges restricted or revoked?

Probably not.

Look at the big picture, and do what's right for your business. Don't let personal feelings knock you down.

11. Take some extra time off—just for the heck of it. Selling on eBay is demanding. Customers are after you 24 / 7. You're rushing to list new items and to ship old ones before your 24-hour deadline expires. Take a break now and then to make time for yourself.

Selling on eBay is tough. It never stops. There's always one more item to list, one more package to mail, and one more email to answer.

It'll tear the hell out of you if you let it, and make you old before your time.

Be sure to schedule some time for yourself before you become the ogre in your basement dungeon.

12. Sell for charity.

eBay Giving Works makes it easy to sell for charity. Pick a national charity like the Red Cross, or choose a local charity that's close to your heart.

Add two or three charity auctions to your repertoire every month. It'll make you feel better about selling on eBay. It'll make your customers feel better about buying from you, and it'll make you more money.

Not every charity Giving Works listing sells or sells for a higher price, but they do get a lot of page views. My listings receive twenty to twenty-five page views. When I add a charity to the listing, it draws several hundred page views, especially when I list using a large national charity.

Even when the item doesn't sell, that's a lot of new eyes on my listings. Many of those lookers take a peek through my eBay store; some of them are likely to pick up an item or two as they're cruising through.

If you haven't tried it yet, list a couple of your items with eBay Giving Works. It just might become a habit.